AL JASSAR

Y0-CDK-123

Balthazar Korab

Alexandra Timchula

More Places for People

Haupt Conservatory,
New York Botanical Garden, page 90

Applied Photography

Clockwise from above:
Millcroft Inn, page 72
Ojai Valley Inn, page 46
Visitors' Center, Chicago Horticultural Society, page 98
Mississippi Queen Steamboat, page 50

Marvin Rand

Julius Shulman

Nick Wheeler

Bill Remington

Chuck Hawley

Clockwise from above:
Olympic Center, Lake Placid, page 176
Harborplace, page 114
Casa Marina Inn, page 28
Ainsworth Gym, Smith College, page 150
Arizona Biltmore, page 34

Clemens Kalischer

Nick Wheeler

Steven Brooke

Norman McGrath

Citicorp Center, page 124

More Places for People

EDITED BY CHARLES K. HOYT, AIA

An Architectural Record Book   McGraw-Hill Book Company

New York St. Louis San Francisco Auckland Bogota Hamburg Johannesburg London Madrid Mexico
Montreal New Dehli Panama Paris Sao Paulo Singapore Sydney Tokyo Toronto

The articles in this book were written by
the editors of *Architectural Record*.

Editors for the book were Patricia Markert
and Joan Zseleczky. The designer was
Anna Egger-Schlesinger. Production
supervisors were Carol Frances and Sally Fliess.

Printed and bound by the Halliday
Lithograph Corporation.

Copyright © 1983 by McGraw-Hill, Inc.
All rights reserved. Printed in the United
States of America. No part of this
publication may be reproduced, stored in a
retrieval system, or transmitted, in any
form or by any means, electronic,
mechanical, photocopying, recording, or
otherwise, without the prior written
permission of the publisher.

1234567890   HDHD   8908765432

Library of Congress Cataloging in Publication Data
Main entry under title:

More places for people.

  "An architectural record book."
  Includes index.
  1. Architecture and recreation—United States—
Addresses, essays, lectures. 2. United States—
Public buildings—Addresses, essays, lectures.
I. Hoyt, Charles King. II. Architectural record.
NA2543.R43M6   725   82-15255
ISBN 0-07-030611-7   AACR2

Contents

The places in this book are places for people's enjoyment. And there never can be enough of them. So the reader who has perhaps read *Architectural Record's* first volume on this subject, *Places for People,* could be left to ponder the true meaning of this book's title. This editor would prefer emphatically that *More Places for People,* be interpreted as a battle cry in advocating more places for people and not just a convenient title for a sequel.

Of course, any manmade construction should brighten people's lives with delight in its appearance and function. Every building should be a place for people. But for the purposes of this book, the description is limited to those constructions which people enjoy when they are at leisure. Even so, there is a wide variety of projects, just as there is a wide variety of leisure activities. Each type is grouped by chapter, so that the reader may focus on it, compare the specific examples, and see why each is successful in meeting a particular set of circumstances, needs and criteria. It is no accident that the locations are all over this country, that some examples are in cities and some in rural areas, that some are very new and modern and some reuse existing buildings in creative ways. In fact there is great variety within each chapter, just as there is a great variety of circumstances, needs and criteria. What unites all of the projects in this book is the common purpose of making our lives more enjoyable.

Some, such as hotels and urban marketplaces, fulfill highly practical and commercial functions as well. And some, such as restaurants and resorts, are limited to that segment of the public which can afford them. But most, such as parks and youth centers (and urban marketplaces and the new town-square-type hotel lobbies as well) are there for everyone to enjoy.

Another attribute shared by all of the varied projects in this book is that they work. That is, they not only set the stage for pleasurable pursuits, they encourage them through basic good planning and by the careful consideration of a host of practical matters—such as durable finishes and adequate exits. The fact that each functions so well, as the builders intended, is a large part of the individual story told with each example.

There are mutual design concerns for each project type which are of interest to the users and instructive to the designers and owners of future facilities. For instance, hotels and restaurants rely for some part of their success on conveying a design message about their intended clientele. (Most simply put, bare-bones furnishings and glaring lights are not consistent with a luxury establishment.)

Resort hotels especially rely on conveying a message about a particular location. (No one wants to feel that she or he is in Cairo when the locale is really in Hawaii.) The right design message often involves more attention to illusion and atmosphere than architects are associated with providing. Accordingly, it is rewarding to see in this book the high level of accomplishment in this area. The reader will be able to spot many more mutual design concerns among the projects in each chapter.

The chapter introductions are designed to give some prospective on how our perception of the various building types changes by briefly examining what the buildings would have been had they been conceived in earlier times. If nothing else, the descriptions point out one of the principal values of this book — keeping the reader abreast of current developments. For some readers, the brief historical descriptions may also point out values that are worth re-examining. They will show how enduring values are translated into new construction, design and social climates.

Introduction

The hotels in this chapter were clearly not meant for the poor, but most provide something for everyone. Until about the time of World War II the grand hotel was equipped with luxurious rooms, spacious lobbies, elegant restaurants and the large service staffs that made everything function in concert with grand intentions. Such places were community centers for local "people of means"—as well as accommodation for those passing through. Those with less substantial means might discreetly position themselves in lobby chairs to watch the arrivals for debutante balls and formal dinners, but the public was not really welcome.

With the demise of large staffs, debutante balls and a lot of decorum, an accommodating (and considerably more democratic) form of hotel elegance has been produced by architects. It relies on spatial concepts—often soaring central atriums that extend up many stories to the roof. These new lobbies are planned on various levels, and have waterfalls, plants and such novelties as glass-enclosed elevators with twinkling lights that move up and down with the cabs. Moreover, the restaurants and bars open directly into these major spaces, producing a new air of accessibility. The drama of such spaces transcends the casual demeanor of staff and guests alike. If the consequence of full-height atriums is rooms opening directly off of the lobby and a resulting lack of privacy, few seem to complain; the effect is exciting theater.

Full of moving, vibrant activity from throngs of the watched and the watching, the new lobby attracts guests—and by no accident, rounds out a self-sufficient environment for that prevalent new social activity, the convention. The conventioneer, lone business-person or tourist need never go outdoors to feel that he or she has been in the center of local public activity. More important to the public, these new urban spaces welcome the passer-by (no matter how unintentionally), and give new impetus for gathering in a stimulating place that often resembles a small-town square full of moving lights at carnival time.

All of this runs contrary to trends in hotel design that prevailed until as recently as the mid-1970s, when every effort was being made to cut costs of construction and maintenance by cutting public space. In the mid-1970s, one well-known hotel consultant was quoted as saying that room costs of $100 per night were not "in the cards." It was a time of flagging demand for rooms.

Still, architect John Portman with the Hyatt chain had pioneered the atrium some ten years before, and many more examples existed. A large part of the turnaround is due both to a different attitude about the commercial value of these public spaces and to the fact that architects have become increasingly involved in producing a total package, instead of the separate inside-outside approach that once existed. The obvious limitation of specialists, following prescribed formulas to design interiors, was a bland appearance of sameness that owners quickly learned they could not afford if they wanted to compete. Today, the hotel that has at least one soaring space filled with activity is—if not commonplace—no longer surprising. Such activity generated by the flow of people to the various functions in ballrooms, convention facilities and restaurants also generates income, a factor that the retrenchment planners of the mid-century overlooked. On the following pages, there are three hotels that exemplify the new spatial concepts: the Hyatt Regency in Dallas by Welton Becket Associates, the Hyatt Regency in Cambridge by Graham Gund Associates and the Peachtree Plaza in Atlanta by John Portman & Associates. The design of the other two hotels sticks to more traditional concepts, and provides an image of quality in separate public rooms. Each of the five is a strong statement about the role that hotels play in contributing to an urban fabric.

Chapter One

Urban Hotels

TYPICAL GUEST FLOOR

SECOND FLOOR - ATRIUM LEVEL

FIRST FLOOR

HYATT REGENCY DALLAS, TEXAS
Welton Becket Associates

This Hyatt hotel was the first structure completed in the core of the Reunion redevelopment area on the edge of the Dallas central business district, and was developed by the Woodbine Development Corporation on privately owned land. The City of Dallas has developed a Special Events Center near the hotel, and has also hired local architects to restore the nearby Union Terminal Building to its original 1914 design as a transportation center, with the addition of specialty shops; it is connected to the hotel by an underground tunnel. Ten acres of public parks span the Reunion redevelopment, creating the largest greenbelt in the downtown area, to be augmented by a series of waterfalls and reflecting pools. Shuttle bus transportation will be used extensively to link the hotel to downtown and to a parking area which serves the redevelopment area and the business district.

Because of the prominent site the hotel occupies, and the expansiveness of the area around it, the hotel was designed to be an ever-changing visual experience, to be experienced from both near and far. In fact, the mystery and delight begin from miles away, as the structure is seen from cars on the freeways. It is the complete integration of forms and exterior materials that create the building's qualities. The reflective glass facade shimmers with moving and distorted lights from passing cars and adjacent buildings, and as the light of the day changes, it is also mirrored, with the full structure projecting a spectrum of light, color and movement.

Beyond the mirror glass facade, the structure has a scaleless dimension. It is an enormous structure—with 1,000 guest rooms positioned in towers with seven distinct roof heights, the highest tower being 30 stories. These varying heights are mixed with rounded forms at the building's corners and slanted roof lines on the southern elevation.

Structurally, it is also distinguished by its innovative and economical use of steel plate shear walls to stiffen the towers to withstand wind force. The plates were stacked on top of each other between columns only in the narrow (east-west) direction; in some cases two panels were joined horizontally to form a broader wall. Stiffeners were added to some panels due to the stress in the wall. Wind shear is transferred from the shear walls to

Balthazar Korab photos

diagonal bracing on the lower two levels, spread through the floor diaphragm, and collected again in the concrete foundation. There was a combination of reasons for the selection of steel plates rather than concrete, but the two major reasons were that the contractor felt using concrete would lengthen the construction time, and a steel moment-resistant frame would have required a tremendous amount of material. The plates actually reduced the amount of steel in columns and beams because the plates accommodate both lateral wind bracing and vertical forces.

Like other Hyatt Regency hotels, the rooms are arranged around an interior atrium space, this one being 200 feet high, 100 feet wide, and 120 feet deep. It is highlighted by a skylight on the southern elevation cascading down from the top of the atrium, but interrupted by four blocks of special suites on the seventh, eighth, eleventh and twelfth floors (see section). The skylight not only permits natural light to flow into the space, but the six-story-high curtain wall below the seventh floor opens up views toward fountains and trees in the adjacent park.

The geometry of the circle is quite evident in the interior design—from the entry tunnel (opposite) to the organizational pattern in the atrium plaza, to the semicircular atrium balconies, and to the arc of the fountains. Glass elevators rise through the atrium along the north wall with views to the atrium plaza and beyond through the glass wall; at the 19th floor, the elevators emerge from the atrium and continue upward along the exterior face of the building in glass-enclosed shafts.

Included in the over-all hotel project is the adjacent Reunion Tower—a 560-foot-high steel and concrete tower, topped by a geodesic dome that contains a restaurant, bar and observation deck. The tower has been dubbed "the electric dandelion" by locals because of the lights attached to an open web framework around the top sphere. Computer-controlled light shows are possible with changing designs. The observation deck houses a glass-enclosed radio station and some displays in addition to providing a full panorama of Dallas and outlying districts.

HYATT REGENCY HOTEL, Dallas, Texas. Owner: *Hunt Investment Corporation.* Developer: *Woodbine Development Corporation.* Architects: *Welton Becket Associates (Los Angeles office)—Alan Rosen, director; Louis Naidorf, director of design; Victor Chu, project designer; Albert Peterson, project director.* Engineers: *Welton Becket Associates (Los Angeles office) —Richard Troy, director of structural engineering; Nabih Youssef, project structural engineer (structural); Herman Blum Consulting Engineers, Inc. (mechanical/electrical).* Consultants: *Evans & Hillman, Inc. (lighting design); The Richards Group (graphics).* Landscape architects: *Myrick-Newman-Dahlberg, Inc.* Interior design: *Howard Hirsch and Associates.* General contractor: *Henry C. Beck Company.*

The entry tunnel to the Hyatt Regency hotel (above), lined with silver panels and red carpeting, creates an exciting—and unexpected—entrance to the hotel. Its design carries forth the geometry of the sphere, used throughout the atrium space. This tunnel leads guests directly to the long registration desk (below), which also continues the curvilinear shape. As one rises on the central escalator from the lobby to the atrium plaza, the grandness of the space, filled with light and activity, is slowly revealed. The "Park Place" lounge (left) is only one of many seating areas on this level, but it is the closest to the tall curtain wall which is so prominent a design element in the atrium. Nearby is a 20-foot waterfall descending to a pool in the lobby.

HYATT REGENCY CAMBRIDGE, MASSACHUSETTS
Graham Gund Associates

The new Hyatt Regency facing Memorial Drive along the Charles River is one more forceful addition to Cambridge's remarkable skyline. As seen by automobile from Storrow Drive on the Boston side, the city at the river's edge is a rapidly flashing by sequence of compelling silhouettes only insignificantly interrupted by ordinary buildings, which appear more decrepit and feeble in this context than they would in another. It is not easy to design a commercial hotel to hold its own in such distinguished and varied institutional company as the Dunster, Leverett and Peabody Terrace student housing at Harvard, or the domed neo-classic complex and late-sixties Earth Sciences tower at MIT.

Architect Graham Gund began his design of the hotel with the usual range of choices. He could have selected a tower-podium concept with the guest rooms in the tower and the bars, restaurants, lobby, conference rooms, kitchens and shops in the podium. Choosing a tower he would have decided whether to make it a double-loaded slab, or rectangular or circular in shape, with or without a John-Portman-like multi-story atrium. This particular Hyatt, however, was to be a small one. The program called for less than 500 guest rooms (by contrast John Portman's most recent completed hotel, the Detroit Plaza has 1,400 rooms). Little towers on the Cambridge shore are rendered insignificant to the automobile passenger from the Boston side as each of the great institutional complexes just mentioned looms into and recedes from view. It was important that the hotel

be seen and remembered.

Gund decided to make his building stand out on the skyline by shaping it like an attenuated ziggurat stretching along the river. By making the building long, narrow and horizontal, he achieved a strong and memorable image facing the river and Boston. The stepped-back floors and the terraces they overlook form an arresting profile. Some of the facilities usually found in the podium of a standard hotel design have been skillfully inserted into a central 14-story atrium (right and overleaf) including the lobby, a restaurant and full-size trees and fountains. The terraces are located to the north and south of the building affording views either up or down the river. More than half the rooms without terraces face the Boston skyline. Others have inside balconies overlooking the atrium. Located on the lower floors are eleven meeting rooms, a ballroom, reception areas and an exhibition area totalling 14.5 thousand square feet.

HYATT REGENCY CAMBRIDGE, Cambridge, Massachusetts. Owner: *Cambridge Hyatt Joint Venture.* Architects: *Graham Gund Associates, Inc.*—partner-in-charge: *Graham Gund;* project manager: *David Mehlin;* project architect: *Peter E. Madsen.* Consultants: *LeMessurier Associates/SCI* (structural); *Cosentini Associates* (mechanical and electrical); *Bolt, Beranek & Newman, Inc.* (acoustical); *William Lam Associates* (lighting); *Jutras & Nicholson Associates* (interiors); *Carol Johnson & Associates* (landscape); *Firepro, Inc.* (fire protection); *Group One Inc.* (kitchens). General contractor: *Vappi & Company, Inc.*

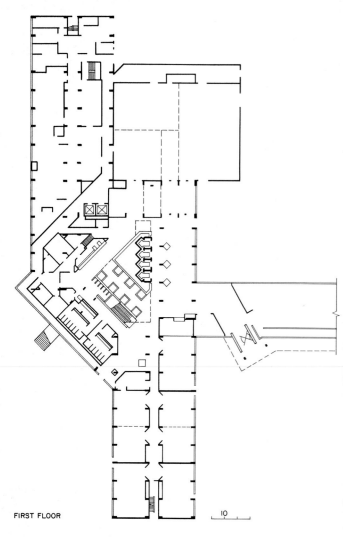

FIRST FLOOR   10

The atrium brings to mind the great interior space of the Larkin building by Frank Lloyd Wright and the glass-enclosed elevators recall his triangulated decoration. The 100-foot-high glass wall braced by space frames (another attractive triangulation) overlooks the Charles River and the Boston skyline. The introduction of natural light from a great window, rather than from the usual skylight, makes the illumination less even but more dramatic. This atrium is an immensely attractive and cheerful place, unimposing and friendly.

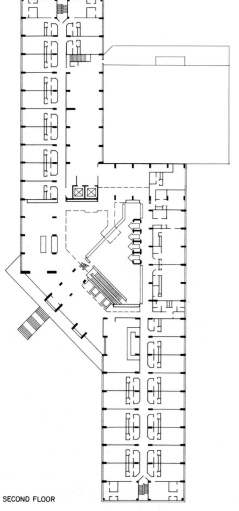

SECOND FLOOR

The rooftop lounge (above and visible in the exterior photo on page 8) slowly revolves 360 degrees, giving its guests a panoramic view of Boston and Cambridge. This feature, like exposed all-glass elevators, appears more and more frequently in luxury hotels as a lure to the potential customer. The restaurants overlooking the atrium are equally attractive.

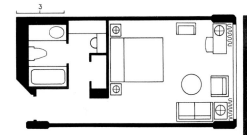

When the closet door in the standard bedroom is open, it closes the dressing room adjacent to the bathroom as shown in the plan (above) and the photo (below). At right is the living room and terrace of a typical suite.

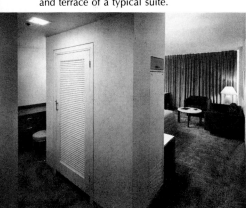

Steve Rosenthal photos

HOTEL MERIDIEN, HOUSTON, TEXAS, Lloyd Jones Brewer Associates

"Intimacy of scale, grandeur of style" were the qualities sought by Air France's subsidiary Meridien Hotels, Inc. for its first venture into the United States market—a luxury hotel which is aimed with Gallic directness to an international, upper-level executive clientele. The location in Allen Center, a business and commercial complex in booming downtown Houston, was chosen for its accessibility to the target market—12 million square feet of prime office space within three blocks, its site amenities—an adjacent park and extensive landscaping within the complex, and a design-development team in full sympathy with Meridien's aim of founding an exclusive first-class hotel in the Continental manner.

At 363 rooms the hotel is small enough, the operators say, to allow personal service but large enough to support fine restaurants. The 19-story trapezoidal tower contains 16 floors of guest rooms rising above a low base that houses below-grade parking and service

areas topped by two levels of public and meeting spaces which extend inward on the site, forming a link with adjacent office and retail spaces. The tower was shaped to maximize the number of rooms fronting the park and designed to contrast in texture as well as geometry with the buff-colored concrete of surrounding structures. The prominent western facade is clad in silver-bronze reflective glass that modulates to bronze-tinted glass on the remaining elevations in a subtle tonal shift that effectively asserts the tower's sharply angular form.

It is in the public spaces, however, that the sought-for "intimacy with grandeur" becomes evident, announcing itself first through what is not there: no atrium, no self-consciously dramatic interior volumes. Instead, the interiors offer what architect Benjamin Brewer characterizes as planned complexity. The reception level is well ordered, and its spatial organization around a visual

axis leading from the sheltered lobby entrance to the landscaped courtyard opposite is at once intricate and readily comprehended. And while the principal activity centers within—reception area and restaurants, bars and boutiques—are distinctly individual, even assertive in character, the potential for discord among them has been overridden by the common denominators of taste and quality to achieve a harmony that Brewer describes as "continuity through contrast."

HOTEL MERIDIEN HOUSTON, Houston, Texas. Owner: *Century Development Corporation.* Operator: *Meridien Hotels, Inc.* Architects: *Lloyd Jones Brewer Associates*—Benjamin E. Brewer, Jr., principal-in-charge; Elmo Valdes, project designer; Russell Reynolds, project director. Interior designers: *Guillon, Smith, Marquart & Associates.* Consultants: *The SWA Group* (landscape); *Ellisor & Tanner* (structural); *Herman Blum Consulting Engineers* (mechanical). Contractor: *Miner-Turner Joint Venture.*

©Richard Payne photos

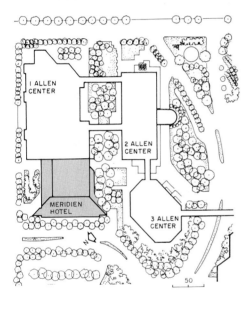

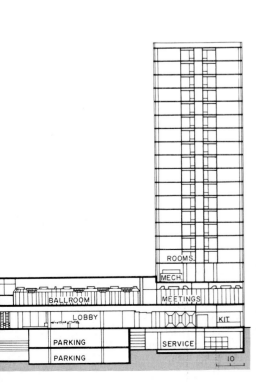

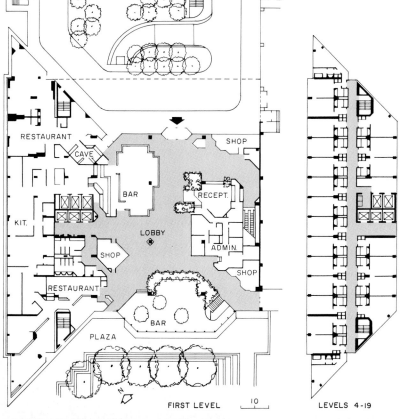

FIRST LEVEL   10   LEVELS 4-19

In a discreet nod to its absent atrium, the Meridien Houston's lobby level features a two-story glass-enclosed garden bar (opposite) that bows outward to a landscaped plaza, its casual furniture and abundant greenery smoothing the transition between more formal interior spaces and the exterior courtyard. On the mezzanine above, a spacious and well-appointed lounge serves as antechamber to the ballroom and other meeting and banquet facilities.

Within the lobby proper a tone of understated elegance is set by the choice of materials—marble floors and column cladding, polished wood paneling, touches of brass and glass. The concierge's station adjoining the reception area (no queuing at registration counters here) is given high visibility by a canopy underhung with a festive array of incandescent globes. Opposite it is a jewel-like cocktail lounge (above) strikingly partitioned by panels of travertine bordered in lacquer and brass. (The fabric scrolls overhead focus lighting and absorb sound.) And in a typical change of key, a seating oasis (right) provides an unobtrusive setting for a 17th-century French tapestry.

PEACHTREE PLAZA HOTEL ATLANTA, GEORGIA
John Portman & Associates

Conceptually, Peachtree Plaza is a round peg in a square hole. The round peg is a cylindrical tower, 70 stories high, which is clad in reflecting glass. The top three floors are given over to a revolving restaurant and cocktail lounge, then there are 56 floors of bedrooms. The views are spectacular. The hotel is the tallest building in Atlanta, and it stands on the highest point in the central area of the city. The square hole, actually a rectangle, is a terraced opening in the seven-story base building, an understated concrete block designed to blend inconspicuously with the other commercial buildings fronting on Peachtree Street. This low building contains the ballrooms, meeting rooms, specialty restaurants and major public spaces of the hotel.

The architectural drama that people have come to expect from Portman is created by the process by which the round peg enters the rectangular hole. The mirrored sides of the tower appear to rest on a two-story concrete collar—containing meeting rooms—whose bottom edge is about 30 feet above the roof level of the base building. Below the collar all the rooms of the tower are stripped away, leaving only the supporting column structure, some narrow balcony walkways, and the elevator core. The opening in the base building that receives the tower is terraced, so that it is wider at the top. The space surrounding the tower within the base building is roofed with domed skylights set in a steel-framed structure. Because of the transition from circle to rectangle, these skylights form a warped plane, although this fact is not readily apparent from inside the building or from the street. If you go up to the swimming pool level, however, and look out over the roof of the main space, you see its curving cellular structure.

The floor of the main space is covered by a reflecting pool, which the hotel's advertising refers to as a half-acre lake. The tower is connected to the rest of the building by bridges at each level, and, at the base of the tower, boat-shaped islands are pushed out between the columns, forming places to have a drink and observe the space and the people.

Access to the roof-top restaurant is by two elevators that run in a glassed-in tube up the exterior of the tower. These elevators are entered at the fifth level, and the elevator structure is supported by a single cylindrical column that comes down into one quadrant of the main space. Another similar elevator structure on the opposite side of the building gives access to the meeting rooms located in the "collar."

The Peachtree Street entrance to the hotel leads you down a very long and narrow corridor, with shops opening off it on either side. The corridor is actually a bridge, and you can look down from it and catch glimpses of the space below—but it is deliberately extremely constricted. At the end of this entrance corridor is a wall, hung with a tapestry, that acts as a baffle. Only when you walk around this wall

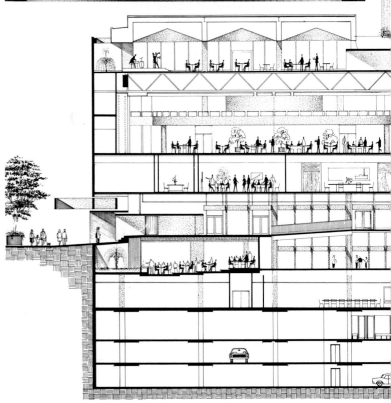

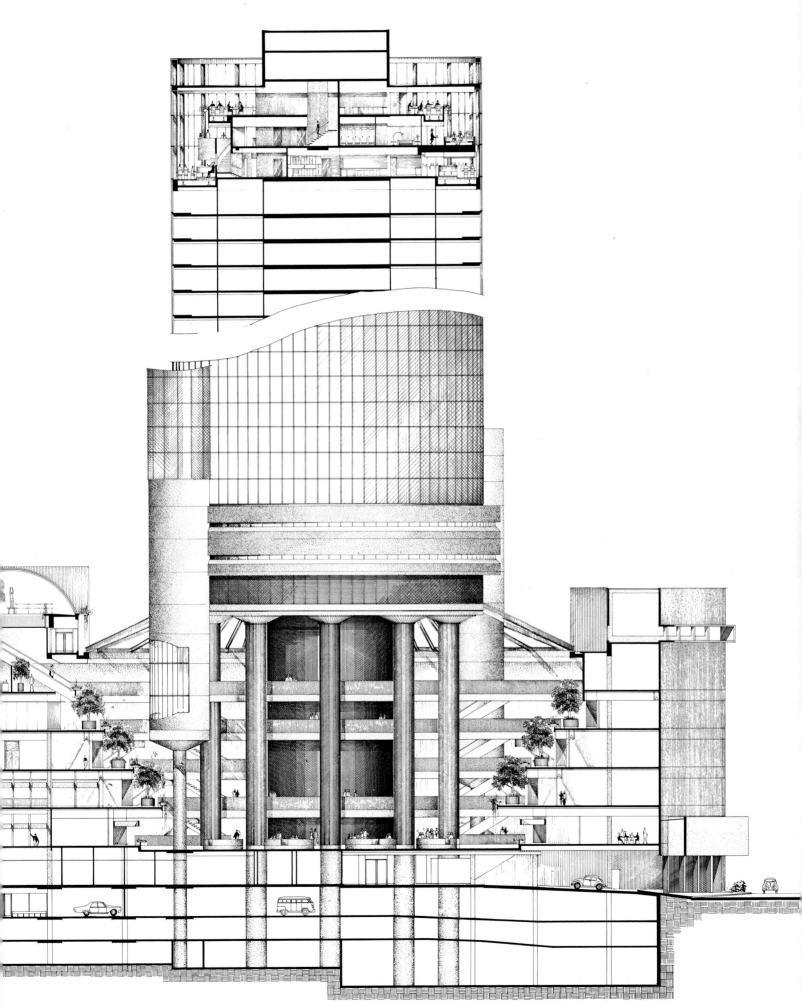

*Above left: afternoon sun streaming down into the south
side of the space. Below, the "lake" level at night,
showing one of the "cocktail islands," intimate areas
from which the life of the surrounding levels
can be observed.*

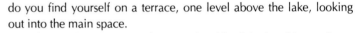

do you find yourself on a terrace, one level above the lake, looking out into the main space.

The motor entrance on the opposite side of the hotel is two floors lower, as the grade drops sharply away from Peachtree Street. From the motor entrance, an escalator brings you up facing the reception desk. You don't catch a glimpse of the water, and the large space opening above it, until you turn away from the desk.

The exterior of the hotel is most impressive from a distance; the cylindrical mirrored tower dominates the Atlanta skyline. The three restaurant floors near the top have bronze tinted windows rather than the reflecting glass that covers the mechanical floor above and the bedroom floors below. The strip of non-reflecting glass makes a subtle termination for the tower, giving something of the feeling of a band of ornament at the top of a column.

Portman has used a quite similar effect at the top of the Fort Worth National Bank building, an octagonal office building covered in reflecting glass, which dominates the Fort Worth skyline in much the same way that the Peachtree Plaza hotel sets its mark on Atlanta.

The main space of the Peachtree Plaza is related to Portman's design for the much larger Bonaventure Hotel in Los Angeles, and to the space connecting the hotel and office buildings of the Renaissance Center in Detroit.

All four of these projects reflect a new departure in Portman's work: making the distinction between public and private space horizontally, rather than vertically. In this way Portman can keep the compactness and efficiency of a tower design, but have a sufficiently impressive space, shared by many different uses, at the base of the tower. (One problem with a 23-story hotel atrium: it's a long way around for room service.) This is not to say that Portman has given up the idea of using major spaces. His recently completed merchandise mart in Brussels has such a space, so does his Apparel Mart in Atlanta.

Portman himself has no need to be imprisoned by the "formula" that he helped create, because he understands the forces that made his original design successful. A point often overlooked in analyzing his architecture is that Portman is also a real-estate developer. When the Peachtree Plaza Hotel opened, *The New York Times* ran a highly favorable analysis by its architectural critic, Paul Goldberger, and a long news story which never once mentioned that Portman Properties

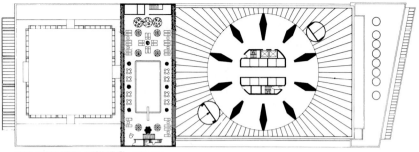

SWIMMING POOL DECK LEVEL

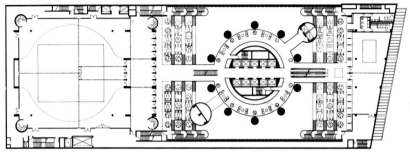

BALLROOM LEVEL

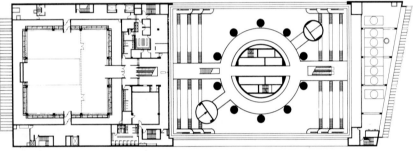

BANQUET LEVEL

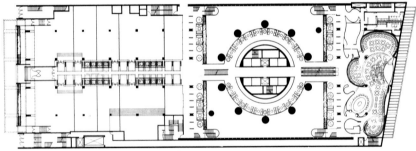

PEACHTREE STREET LEVEL

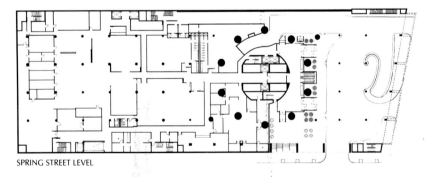

SPRING STREET LEVEL

MAIN LOBBY LEVEL

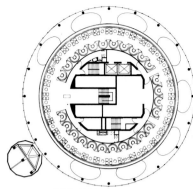

ROOFTOP COCKTAIL LEVEL

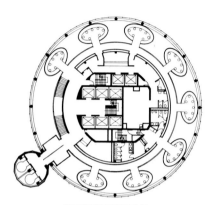

ROOFTOP ENTRY LEVEL

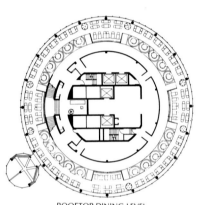

ROOFTOP DINING LEVEL

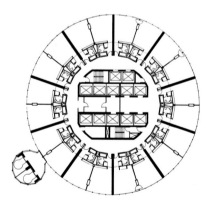

TYPICAL BEDROOM FLOOR

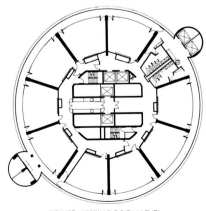

TOWER MEETING ROOM LEVEL

20

The island motif of the main space is repeated at the intermediate level of the roof-top restaurant. The top level is a circular cocktail lounge with a revolving platform. The dining level also revolves. At intervals you find yourself under one of the island-like structures and then out into the full three stories, so that your space changes as well as the view.

was the developer for the hotel and that Portman interests own it. The point is an important one, because the budget for the hotel is determined by the market place, not by a corporation looking for "prestige" or a non-profit institution that is not thinking in investment terms.

The Atlanta Regency went against all the conventional wisdom of hotel design at the time that it was planned. It is highly unlikely that it would have been built if Portman hadn't put together the backing for it (it was purchased from the original developers by Hyatt before the hotel was completed). Portman evoked Tivoli to compete with the downtown motor hotels, notoriously un-amusing places to stay. With his new hotel he had a different problem: how to compete with the Regency, and with three other new hotels in Atlanta, which have what could be called Portmanesque spaces.

The atmosphere of the new Peachtree Plaza evokes a different tradition: that of the "palace" hotel. Its public areas are luxurious and the spaces have a Roman grandeur. The hotel is also full of ornamental touches that most other architects would be too inhibited to use. Long chains of diamond-shaped figures cut out of aluminum hang alongside the columns of the main space. Chains of clear plastic globes hang from the ceiling of the roof-top restaurant. Canopies of beaded fringe define seating areas and restaurant tables. The test is to imagine what the spaces would be like without them. It is clear that Portman knows what he is doing.

The Peachtree Plaza Hotel is not an isolated project. It is part of Peachtree Center, an inter-connected group of buildings which have all been developed by Portman and most of which are still owned by business entities that Portman controls. Besides the Regency and Peachtree Plaza Hotels, there are five office buildings, a 2-million-square-foot Merchandise Mart, two parking garages, an enclosed shopping mall, a dinner theater, and an Apparel Mart. The Peachtree Center complex is also starting to tie in with the rest of downtown Atlanta. Davison's department store now opens directly into the lobby of the Peachtree Plaza.

Peachtree Center functions as what Portman calls a "co-ordinate unit" whose different parts all reinforce each other. The trade shows at the Mart help create a need for hotel rooms, the restaurants in the hotels also serve the office buildings and mart, the shops serve all three major uses, drawing people for their own sakes as well, and so on . . .

PEACHTREE PLAZA HOTEL, Atlanta, Georgia. Owner: *Peachtree Hotel Company.* Architects, structural engineers, and interior designers for the public spaces: *John Portman & Associates, Architects and Engineers.* Interior design for guest rooms and back of house: *Western Service and Supply Corporation.* Engineers: *Britt Alderman Associates* (mechanical); *Morris E. Harrison & Associates* (electrical). Consultants: *William C. Lam* (lighting); *J. R. Ballantine & Associates, Inc.* (acoustical). Contractor: *J. A. Jones Construction Company.*

At right, the "Terrace Room" restaurant, where space is defined by banners. The soffits into which the banners fit are an integral part of the structure, evidence that for Portman every step in the creation of a building—from first concept to interior design details—is part of the same process. Above: one of the suites at the top of the tower showing the airplane-like view. The decor of the hotel rooms is the work of Western International's own staff, in consultation with the Portman organization. Western International is the operator of the hotel.

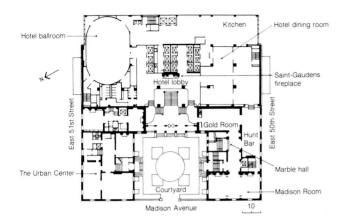

THE VILLARD HOUSES
HELMSLEY PALACE HOTEL
NEW YORK CITY
McKim, Mead & White
Restored by Emery Roth & Sons

SAINT-GAUDENS FIREPLACE IN THE LOBBY

Steven Zane photos

Preservationists girded for battle in 1974 when plans for grafting a high-rise hotel onto New York's landmark Villard Houses threatened to destroy some of the finest domestic interiors in the city. Designed in 1882 by McKim, Mead & White for railroad tycoon Henry Villard, and subsequently the home of publisher Whitelaw Reid, the south wing of the group of neo-Renaissance brownstones (across Madison Avenue from St. Patrick's Cathedral) boasts decor by Stanford White, sculpture by Augustus Saint-Gaudens, and murals by John La Farge, as well as exquisite stained glass, mosaics, plasterwork, and marquetry. Fortunately, developer Harry B. Helmsley, who leased the site from the Catholic Archdiocese of New York, was convinced that the belle-époque grandeur of the Villard interiors was an irreplaceable asset for his new Palace. All of the major rooms in the south wing have not only been incorporated into the hotel, but restored to gilt-edged splendor.

The task for interweaving old and new fabric presented the architect, Emery Roth & Sons, with a complex challenge. Extreme care was required to reinforce and protect fragile turn-of-the-century interiors during construction of the 51-story hotel tower. Ingenious planning by James W. Rhodes, Roth's project architect for renovation, salvaged decorative elements endangered by interior demolition. Individual fragments became pieces in a movable puzzle, much of which was reassembled within the new hotel. The most conspicuous transplant is the monumental fireplace designed by Saint-Gaudens for the Villard dining room. Displaced when this room was remodeled into the Palace's Hunt Bar, it is now the focus of the Madison Avenue lobby, which occupies the central wing of the U-shaped courtyard. The north wing (not illustrated on these pages) has been converted by James Stewart Polshek and Associates into the Urban Center, headquarters and exhibition space for The Architectural League, The Municipal Art Society, and the New York City Chapter of AIA.

Before construction of the hotel began, an historic structures report was prepared by consultant William C. Shopsin, AIA, and painstaking graphic documentation, supervised by James Rhodes, recorded all extant components of the Villard Houses for the Historic American Buildings Survey. (Even though the Villard-Reid mansion had been adapted for use as diocesan offices and meeting rooms during the 1940s, most of the original fabric survived intact.) Various photographic techniques, including photogrammetry, a process developed during the Second World War for aerial plotting of terrain, provided the basis for detailed drawings. All movable items—from switchplates to chandeliers—were inventoried and placed in storage. A number of portable elements had already been lost to "sophisticated looters," according to William Weber of Rambusch, the decorating company which carried out much of the restoration and made facsimiles of missing objects. Vulnerable ornament that had to remain in place, such as coffered plaster soffits, was molded in rubber for later duplication in the new structure. Foam-topped shoring stood ready to catch ornamental ceilings; and padded, fireproof plywood shields encased delicate cabinet work and decorative masonry. As a final precaution against tremors from blasting and drilling, on-site observers kept close watch on seismic monitors.

Once the dust had cleared, teams of artisans began piecing the puzzle back together. "We always took the course of least interference," says architect Rhodes, "Just brushing off or cleaning whenever possible, and restoring or replacing only where it could not be avoided." The most impressive cleaning job was performed in the Villard entry hall, a marble-walled staircase and loggia embellished with opalescent leaded glass, mosaic floors and ceilings, and a zodiacal clock in bas-relief, designed by Saint-Gaudens. Application of solvents, poultice, and polish restored the inlaid surfaces to lapidary purity. Different cleaning techniques were needed for the Hunt Bar ceiling, which is clad in elaborate panels of molded Lincrusta, an oil-based papier-mâché used by Victorian decorators to simulate tooled leather.

The filigree of Stanford White's barrel-vaulted ceiling in the Music Room (now the Gold Room, where breakfast, tea, and cocktails are served) was regilded with three different finishes to replicate the original spectrum of tones: 13- and 23-karat gold leaf, and Dutch metal (a compound of brass and copper). Harry Helmsley "got carried away with the beauty of the Gold Room," says his wife

THE GOLD ROOM (ABOVE); THE MADISON ROOM (BELOW)

LIBRARY CEILING DETAIL (ABOVE); HALL CLOCK (BELOW)

Leona, president of Helmsley Hotels. "He told the workmen not to baby the gold leaf, but to use as much as they could." Armorial stained-glass casements had always been the chief source of illumination for the glittering reliefs, but now faced a solid wall of the new tower. In order to avoid the even glare of artificial back-lighting, which "killed" the subtle texture of the glass, white boxes behind the windows were lined with crumpled aluminum foil, whose reflection approximates the scintillation of sunlight. Additional lights were mounted at cornice level to enhance the clarity of two newly-cleaned lunette murals by John La Farge. Figurative roundels by academic painter George W. Breck on the water-damaged ceiling of Whitelaw Reid's library (now a conference room) were also restored, along with plaster coffers studded with the colophons of famous publishers.

Recreating the French Classical elegance of the main drawing room (now the Madison Room, a cocktail lounge) involved James Rhodes and interior designer Sarah Lee, of Tom Lee, Ltd., in a formidable game of hide-and-seek. Removal of built-in office cabinets revealed superb onyx chimneypieces, and a marble niche turned out to be hinged for use as a secret door (formerly a discreet exit for the bored host, it now connects to a fire stair). Fan-coil units, which elsewhere in the building are tucked inside antique chests or behind shutters or wall paneling, are here concealed below marbleized windowsills. Upholstery fabric, hangings, and rugs had to be ordered to match marble veneers whose glaucous hue changed markedly as additional layers of grime were rubbed away. The original furnishings of the house had long since been dispersed, and the Helmsleys and Sarah Lee agreed that an archaeological replica of all original fittings would be a futile—and impractical—exercise of scholarship. Instead, they sought to evoke the aura of the Gilded Age without disappointing the expectations of present-day hotel guests. "We had to respect the treasures of the Villard House, but we knew we weren't doing a museum display," says Mrs. Lee. "Photographs survive of the interiors when they were first installed, and people would be appalled by the heavy draperies, deep valances, and fringes that all seem so depressing today. I have a hunch that it's prettier now than it was when the house first opened."

THE HELMSLEY PALACE HOTEL, New York, New York. Architects: *Emery Roth & Sons, P.C.—Richard Roth, Jr., partner-in-charge; John Secreti, project architect; Vijay Kale, designer; James W. Rhodes, project architect for the renovation.* Engineers: *Irwin G. Cantor* (structural/foundation); *Meyer, Strong & Jones, P.C.* (mechanical/electrical); *Cerami and Associates, Inc.* (acoustical); *Howard Brandston Lighting Design, Inc.* (lighting). Interior design: *Tom Lee, Ltd.—Sarah Lee, executive designer; Warren McCurtain, project designer.* General contractor and cost consultant: *Morse/Diesel, Inc.* Subcontractor for interior restoration: *Rambusch* (plasterwork, painting, marble, mosaics, gold leaf); *John Langenbacher Co., Inc.,* (woodwork); *Remco* (marble).

As a different kind of place for people, successful resorts offer more varied attractions in more spread out facilities than the new urban hotels with their concentrated, inward focus. A resort's guests generally arrive for longer stays, and they want to be lulled into relaxation by many kinds of activities, not only indoors but outdoors as well. No matter how dramatic the main lobby may be, there will be many public rooms for everything from reading to athletic pursuits—as well as a direct relationship to the attractions without. In fact, a critical ingredient of success will be how well a resort capitalizes on its particular location—be it beach, forest or mountains. The real focus is outward. Accordingly, the match of facilities to a particular location becomes a critical matter for close examination. The mud rooms, large fireplaces and ski rental facilities for a resort in the mountains are very different from the poolside bars, showers and cabana-rental facilities at the beach.

Similarly, the character of the buildings needs special attention for several reasons that include taking advantage of the natural location by not intruding too heavily upon it. Who really wants to take the city in the shape of an urban tower to the ski slope—not to mention the ungainly effect on the landscape that such a building would produce? The most pleasurable resorts from all points of view will generally be low rise, and fit into their surroundings as unobtrusively as possible. The Ojai Valley Inn by Peter Gluck & Associates is an outstanding example in this chapter.

Another important reason to consider character is to give the guests a sense of being somewhere special in a unique locale — a sense that will enhance their enjoyment while they play, and encourage thoughts of return when they are gone. For many architects and designers, this will mean keeping the design language of the new facilities as simple as possible, background design that lets the surroundings speak for themselves. On the following pages, an addition to the Casa Marina Inn in Key West by Peter L. Gluck & Associates and the New Harmony Inn by Woollen Associates are outstanding examples of this approach.

Other successful designs will incorporate more literal references to local character, while avoiding the trite, the ersatz and the over-contrived. And it is rewarding to see that architects are now successfully embracing such concepts after many years of grappling. Still, the most comfortable way that modern architects can produce regional flair is through the renovation of older existing facilities. Such projects often have benefits for the owners in addition to their unique character; they are often cheaper to produce, and often win the good will of a local population happy to see tradition restored instead of another new intrusion in the community. On these pages, the restoration of the original part of the Casa Marina noted earlier and the restoration of the Arizona Biltmore, by the Frank Lloyd Wright Foundation, each produce a very memorable, valuable and regionally appropriate cultural contribution — as well as a delightful, nostalgic and profitable one. The reconstruction of the Mississippi Queen Steamboat by Albert P. Hinckley Jr. falls in a class by itself—a moving piece of architecture suffused with nostalgia.

With the high cost per room of building a resort (due to all of its special facilities for relaxation) and the high cost of running it (due to the large staffs), an owner can hardly afford to let his guests down on the design of the physical environment. Guests come with a heightened anticipation of the experience that awaits them, and the successful owner will make sure that they get what they expect.

Chapter Two

Resort Hotels and Inns

CASA MARINA INN
KEY WEST, FLORIDA
Peter L. Gluck & Associates

John Zimmerman

Karen Selsky

At the tip of Florida's southern archipelago, 150 miles from Miami, lies the once sleepy fishing village of Key West. In recent years, the former home to Hemingway has become the tropical playground for sun-seekers from the Northeast. Although the island's fledgling economy depends upon tourism, the throngs of vacationers threatened to overwhelm the facilities—the picturesque conch guesthouses could not absorb the island's newfound popularity and the demand was importunately met by rows of undistinguished chain motels that now blight Key West's palm-lined streets.

But flanking the Atlantic shore of Old Town, Key West, the abandoned Casa Marina Inn (photo left) stood as a reminder of more elegant and leisured days. Opened on New Year's Day, 1921, the hotel was built by railroad magnate Henry Flagler as the southernmost outpost for passengers on his Florida East Coast Railroad. Like Flagler's Breakers Hotel in Palm Beach, and Ponce de Leon Hotel in Saint Augustine, the Casa Marina belongs to the rich tradition of grand hotels, but like many fine old resorts, it has seen some hard

times. During World War II, the hotel was used to house Naval officers and during the Cuban Missile Crisis of 1962, the Army leased the space to house armaments. Since then the resort has served as Army barracks, training site for the Peace Corps, and temporary home to a group of Micronesian refugees. But fate—and the market—have once again smiled on Henry Flagler's endangered behemoth. New York architect Peter Gluck was commissioned to renovate and restore the original 250-room facility, and to design a 139-room addition that would incorporate a convention center. The renovation rescues an important local landmark, and the addition ensures its economic stability. Hard line preservationists would argue that the ideal commission would have been a careful restoration of the Flagler hotel—without the conference center or addition—but the economics of a winter resort hotel are grim for the summer months and convention business guarantees year-round solvency. As with so many market-motivated blends of old and new, the overriding theme seems to be *quid pro quo.*

photos by Steven Brooke except as noted

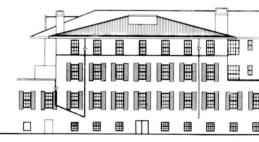

This is not Peter Gluck's first opportunity to explore the problem of juxtaposing a new guest wing with an ''indigenous'' hotel. In his earlier Ojai Valley Inn project (page 46), Gluck carved a 175-room addition into the side of a California hill and then masked the rooms behind trellises covered with flowering vines. The Key West project offered no such novel opportunity but architect Gluck has shown a comparable sensitivity to the context of both the 1921 hotel and bordering Seminole Street.

The addition is at first glance jarring—a striking counterpoint to Flagler's romantic blend of arches and shutters capped with a red tile roof. But this crisp division between the old and the new was precisely what Peter Gluck was after: ''The intention of the new building was to leave the old building, not violate it, not try to ape it or mimic it, but to
30

exist next to it and independently of it so the old building can be seen in its entirety.''

The triangular site and the orientation of the old hotel determined the placement of the addition. The architect regarded ocean views and a generous expanse of open lawn on the Atlantic primary considerations: to secure both, he has pushed the addition to the edge of the site, flush with tiny Seminole Street. In plan it takes on the guise of an oversized ''extension'' to one wing of the old hotel. But the combined width of the 500-foot-wide hotel and the 400-foot-wide addition threatened to overwhelm the site. To reduce the massing of the now 900-foot-wide structure, the addition has been layered back in three parts, and can be glimpsed only in sections as it recedes toward the street. And to make the new wing less rigid as it fronts the street, Gluck has used a facade

reminiscent of Aldo Rossi—sheer wall with seemingly endless rows of perfectly symmetrical windows framed by rows of traditional shutters. According to the program, each room was to be exactly the same; the fenestration serves to remind us of that continuity. Although the street facade is regimented, the shutters counter the severity—one is reminded of New Orleans perhaps.

The old hotel is solid concrete, 14- to 20-inches thick, and the addition is 1-inch stucco. To soften the massive effect of so large a masonry structure, Gluck has used detached screens for the two sections of the new wing that are most highly visible (photo above). The screens were to be built of wood—to distinguish them as *surface*—but that was one of the battles the architect lost with the owners, and the screens are now stucco as well; but even so, they serve to

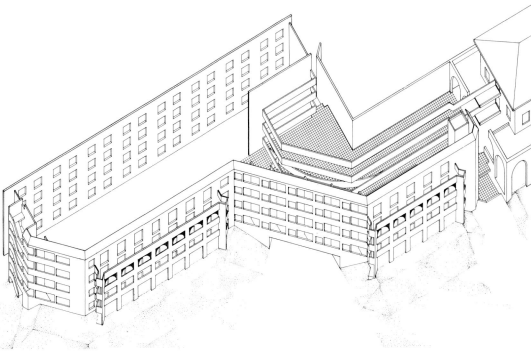

John Zimmerman

The addition picks up the line and scale of the old hotel (photo right). For the future, a condominium is slated for the other side of the street, and when built will serve as a counterpart to the Casa Marina. The architect wanted the street facade to contain traditional elements appropriate for a small sidestreet. The shutters add an associative element to an otherwise *hard* structure. The elevation below shows the regimentation of windows and shutters, and the walkways that connect the three floor old hotel to the four floor addition. The conference center connects the two buildings at street level, and maintains the line of the street.

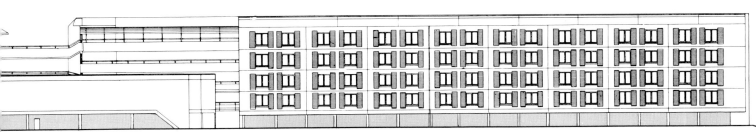

break up the mass, and the spaces between the building and the screens become private balconies. The owners also regarded arches as necessary to relate the new more literally to the old. Gluck has obliged by including lattice arches to frame the balconies on the third floor; like the screens, the arches help to offset the mass of masonry, and, like the shutters of the street facade, add another associative fragment.

Rather than abut the new building into the old, Gluck has left them separate, and they converge at a courtyard. The courtyard relates neither to the old building nor the new; it is instead the axis from which the two buildings pivot. The courtyard is neutral—almost early Modern in style—and according to Gluck serves as passage to modulate the transition from old to new.

The addition takes on a Y-shape as if to

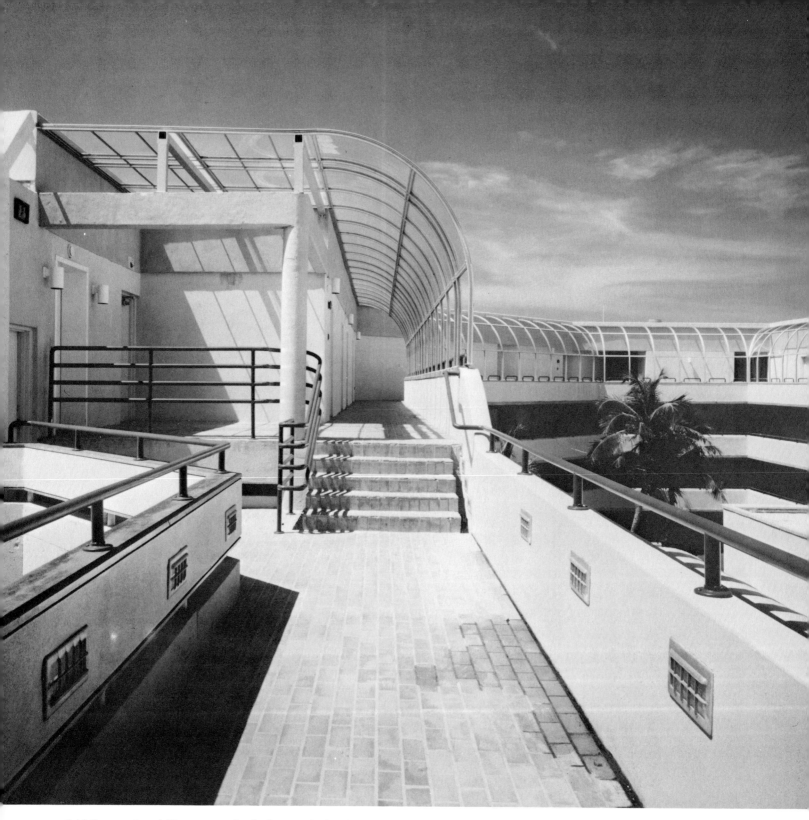

enfold the courtyard. To prevent the feeling of enclosure, Gluck has placed an acrylic plastic awning over the fourth floor corridor (photo above) so when looking up from the interior courtyard, one sees not sheer wall, but rather the eye is naturally drawn at a slant over the fourth floor and through the transparent roof. The curved awning not only echoes the arches of the old hotel, but welcomes sunlight into the courtyard.

For the Flagler hotel, architect Gluck pared down the existing 250 rooms to a more generously proportioned 108. (Originally the rooms measured 8-feet 6-inches wide). The room enlargements necessitated a new system for aligning the unaltered windows. The new plan offers a diversity in room arrangements for the old hotel—a diversity not allowed in the program for the addition.

The commission for the Casa Marina

stipulated that the architect have no control over the hotel interiors—and it shows. It is unfortunate that the owners did not allow the same thoughtful design to invade the hotel; the lobby and the rooms are now filled with the standard "resort" bill-of-fare.

Within the restraints imposed by the program, budget, site, and client, architect Gluck has designed a facility that is responsive to each. But one wishes—and perhaps unrealistically—for fewer restraints.

MARRIOTT'S CASA MARINA INN, Key West, Florida. Owner: *Cayo Hueso Limited Partnership.* Architects: *Peter L. Gluck and Associates—Geoffrey L. Koper, project architect.* Engineers: *Geiger Berger Associates, P.C. (structural); Thomas A. Polise (mechanical/electrical).* General contractor: *Jansen Co. of Florida.* Subcontractors: *Delta Contractors (mechanical/electrical/plumbing).*

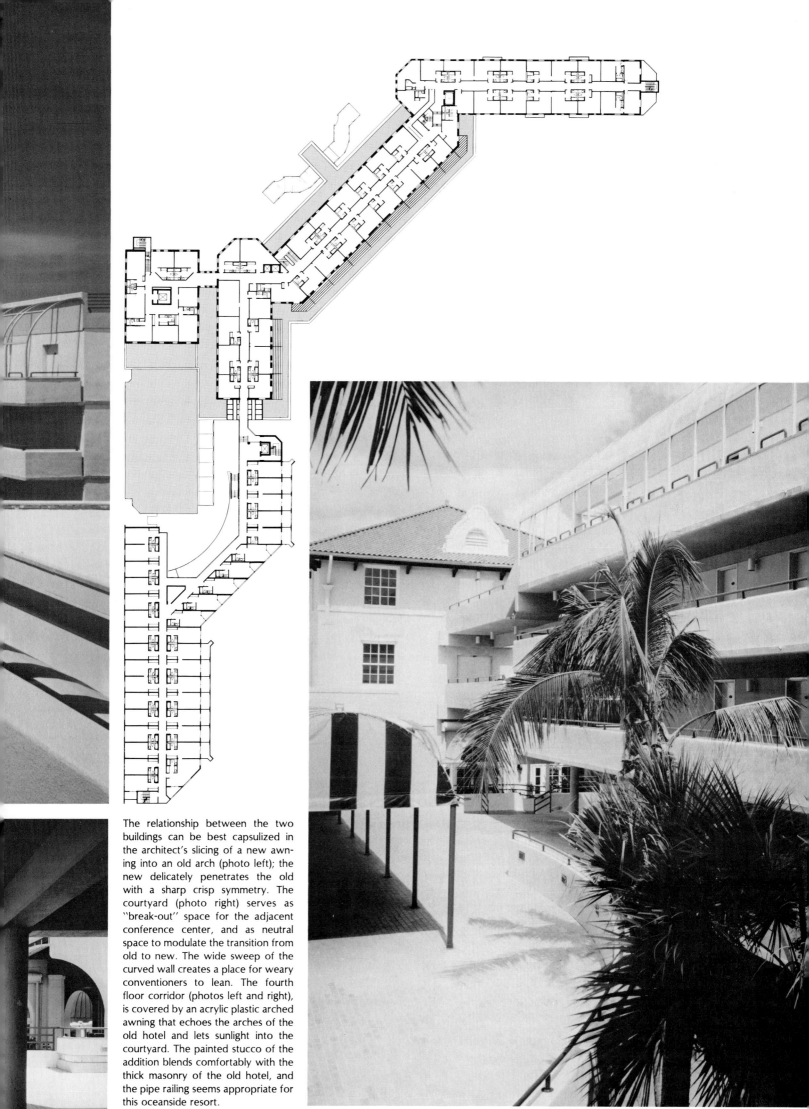

The relationship between the two buildings can be best capsulized in the architect's slicing of a new awning into an old arch (photo left); the new delicately penetrates the old with a sharp crisp symmetry. The courtyard (photo right) serves as "break-out" space for the adjacent conference center, and as neutral space to modulate the transition from old to new. The wide sweep of the curved wall creates a place for weary conventioners to lean. The fourth floor corridor (photos left and right), is covered by an acrylic plastic arched awning that echoes the arches of the old hotel and lets sunlight into the courtyard. The painted stucco of the addition blends comfortably with the thick masonry of the old hotel, and the pipe railing seems appropriate for this oceanside resort.

Chuck Hawley photos except as noted

1 Lobby
2 Orangerie
3 **Aztec Lounge**
4 Ballroom
5 Conference Center 1979
6 Cottages
7 Valley Wing 1979
8 Paradise Wing 1975
9 Pool
10 Foyer

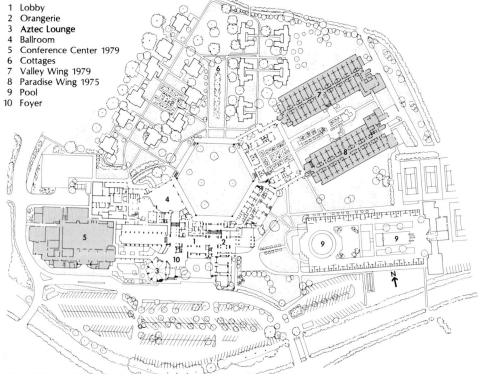

ARIZONA BILTMORE
PHOENIX, ARIZONA
Restored by
The Frank Lloyd Wright
Foundation

Neil Koppes

The 1929 June issue of ARCHITECTURAL RECORD credits Albert Chase McArthur as the architect for the Arizona Biltmore Hotel. But it comes as little surprise to discover that McArthur worked as a draftsman in the Oak Park Studio of Frank Lloyd Wright. When McArthur's two brothers conceived the idea for an elegant resort hotel, they naturally handed the job to their brother, and he in turn naturally requested the assistance of his former mentor. Though Wright must have balked at anything less than top billing, a resort complex in the midst of the Arizona desert would have been an irresistable opportunity to display his theory of "Organic Architecture." And, according to Olgivanna Lloyd Wright, "To spare the destruction of the landscape had in fact been my husband's lifelong thesis in relation to what is now termed environmental planning."

Wright's theories about an architecture synchronized with the landscape could have found no better proving ground than the Arizona Biltmore; the hotel rises discreetly from an arid mesa, and is composed of forms and materials that are clearly derived from the desert terrain and the indigenous flora. In keeping with the spirit and texture of the desertscape, Wright used the humble concrete block as the primary interior and exterior building material. At the time, concrete block was considered the "vulgarian" of the construction industry, but Wright was determined to raise the lowly block to esthetic respectability. The blocks were all molded on site with exquisite details and patterns designed by McArthur and Wright.

The Biltmore opened in February of 1929, and crowned "Jewel of the Desert." Only a few months later the stock market crash brought the Depression and the hotel was purchased by chewing gum magnate William Wrigley, along with 1200 acres of adjacent land. Wrigley saw his role not only as owner, but benefactor—each year the hotel's operating deficit was paid off by a personal check.

Since the halcyon days of Wrigley and the leisure class, the Arizona Biltmore has undergone some dramatic alterations. But with the guidance of John Rattenbury of Taliesin West, Wright's only existing hotel retains its original splendor.

The main building materials for the hotel—copper for the roof, gold for the ceiling, and sand for the concrete block—are all indigenous to Arizona. The Aztec Lounge (right) with its sharply attenuated roof (top) is adjacent to the hotel entrance. The main lobby (below) is reached after first passing through a foyer that contains a symbolic oasis and a 1927 mural by Wright (right). The mural is the architect's abstraction of the desert flora—using the T-square, triangle, and compass to achieve the design. The lighting system is integrated into the structure, as glass intermittently replaces concrete block.

Markow Photography

Neil Koppes

In June of 1973, the Wrigley family sold the Biltmore to Talley Industries; three weeks later, while workmen were updating the sprinkler system, a welder's torch ignited insulation material and a six-alarm fire completely destroyed the fourth floor of the hotel and gutted the interiors. The new owners were determined to reopen September 29, for the winter season, and a feverish reconstruction effort began.

After interviewing several firms, the new owners commissioned Taliesin Associated Architects of the Frank Lloyd Wright Foundation to oversee the construction. To ensure the authenticity of the project, the architects rallied to the cause with Wright's original drawings on linen from the Foundation's vaults. Concrete block was molded on-site using Arizona sand, duplicating the texture and patterns of the original (the 1929 alumi-

num molds were fortunately saved by the owners and fiberglass form liners were fabricated using the original aluminum molds as matrices). New carpets based on six of Wright's geometric patterns from the early 1920s were woven in Ireland, and two workmen from the 1929 construction job were called out of retirement to teach 15 young workers how to apply the more than 38,000-square-feet of gold leaf onto the "largest gold leaf ceiling in the world."

The copper roof posed an especially tricky problem: how to reproduce the patina created by 44 years of Arizona sun. In what must be the surest testimony of the new owner's commitment to the project, Talley Industries' research staff invented a chemical process to produce the desired patina. And after a miraculous 91 days, the hotel was again open for business.

Many of the designs used in the reconstruction were not from the original Biltmore project: the pattern for the lobby carpet was borrowed from the Imperial Hotel in Tokyo, and some of the furniture was designed by Wright in the 1950s. But it is all *bona fide* Wright—re-interpreted, re-colored, and re-applied for the Biltmore. Ironically, the hotel is more *Wrightian* after reconstruction, and the shared credits seem now to favor Wright over McArthur—even if posthumously.

In 1977, a Canadian investment group purchased the hotel, and with the new owners came a major expansion program. A 120-room addition, the Valley Wing, was built parallel to the 90-room Paradise Wing addition, dating from 1975 (photo top, next page). The two new guest wings have been pushed to the side, behind the original structure, and, as designed by the Taliesin archi-

Balthazar Korab

One of the new guest room additions (above) is joined to the original hotel by a covered walkway (top right). The Orangerie cafe/cabaret (below), with its stalactite chandeliers, flanks the main lobby and was added after the 1973 fire to replace a cocktail lounge. The large photo on the right makes evident the architects' painstaking attention to texture, form, and detail. The concrete block, facing the flue of the fireplace, is perforated with glass inserts to expose flames shooting up the chimney. The furniture is casual, overstuffed, almost domestic, and makes a soothing counterpart to the intricate patterns molded into the concrete block. The carpets are patterned after six of Wright's geometric designs.

Balthazar Korab Neil Koppes Markow Photography

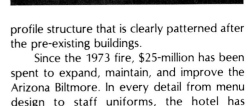

tects, are carefully deferential to the original buildings. Although the additions take their inspiration and materials from Wright, they seem less integrated into the landscape and less shaped by the terrain; instead, they provide a sympathetic backdrop.

Nowhere is the hand of Wright more evident than in the hotel interiors—especially the public spaces. A low concrete portico connects the driveway to a foyer that welcomes guests with a symbolic mini-oasis—a freestanding cluster of columns, plants and a waterfall.

Adjacent to the foyer, the circular Aztec Lounge creates the contextural drama for which Wright is famous. As light filters through the glass-filled perforations in the concrete block of the soffit onto the gold ceiling, the room takes on a spectacular aura. The foyer opens onto a 260-foot-long lobby that serves as the major circulation route for the hotel, leading into restaurants, gardens, and, on each side of the registration desk, to the guest rooms. But the lobby is also one of the more active social areas for the hotel; the scale of the elongated rectangle has been reduced by a mezzanine and small groupings of overstuffed furniture (designed by Wright in the 1950s for Heritage-Henredon, though never manufactured). The lighting system is carefully integrated into the structure, punctuating the columns with opal glass panels shielding metal fixtures on the same module as the concrete block.

All of the guest rooms have been completely refurbished, and each contains a triptych silkscreen adaptation of a Wright mural.

In the fall of last year, a 39,000-square-foot convention center was completed. The Taliesin architects again have designed a low-profile structure that is clearly patterned after the pre-existing buildings.

Since the 1973 fire, $25-million has been spent to expand, maintain, and improve the Arizona Biltmore. In every detail from menu design to staff uniforms, the hotel has received an unparalleled level of attention. The Biltmore remains a brilliant example of "Organic Architecture"—indigenous materials, molded by the landscape, and integrated into a unified complementary whole.

ARIZONA BILTMORE HOTEL, Phoenix, Arizona. Owner: *Rostland Inc.* Architect: *Frank Lloyd Wright Foundation—project architect, John Rattenbury.* Engineers: *Magadini-Alagia Associates (structural); Sergent Hauskins & Beckwith (foundation); Sullivan & Masson (mechanical/electrical).* Consultants: *Frank Lloyd Wright Foundation (interiors/landscape/graphics).* Contractor: *Kitchell Inc.*

Douglas Gillespie

Original Rappite dormitory; below, Inn and "roofless church."

Camera Arts Studio

NEW HARMONY INN
NEW HARMONY, INDIANA
Woollen Associates

Balthazar Korab photos, except as noted

Evans Woollen describes his firm's design for the New Harmony Inn in New Harmony, Indiana, as "situational" architecture—an architecture that makes every effort to be particular to the place where it is built. In this case, the place is a small midwestern town founded in 1814 by a communal sect of German Lutherans who called themselves Rappites. Ten years after the founding, the Rappites, having erected buildings in the manner of the men's dormitory shown in the small photograph above, sold the town outright to Robert Owen, a wealthy cotton mill owner in Scotland, and they moved away. Owen hoped to found a utopian society based on universal education, and, though the communal aspect of his experiment was finally a failure, New Harmony survived as an important intellectual center well into the late nineteenth century. Much more recently, at the instigation of the wife of a descendant of Robert Owen and of architectural historian Ralph G. Schwarz, New Harmony has become the subject of renewed development—the result of a whopping $21 million investment to turn it into an important center for tourism and educational programs (without, it is hoped, the chaotic consequences that sometimes attend such endeavors). This 45-room inn is a major part of the refurbishing. According to Woollen, the first design, for a site just outside the town, was strongly neo-Corbusian. Though it was in the end not built because the land could not be acquired, it elicited strong reaction. "It had a lot of amenities," says Woollen, "but nothing to do with New Harmony; people thought something would be lost if it were built." The town itself has several strong and readily identifiable qualities. The older buildings are no more than three stories high, and the important ones are

George Cserna

made out of brick, while the less important ones are of wood. None of them, moreover, seem quite as memorable as the overall format of the town, which is characterized by streets lined with beautiful old trees.

The inn was designed modestly to reinforce the existing situation. "By virtue of its having been off the beaten track, there is a built-in respect for context in New Harmony," Woollen says. "People in the 1870s went right on building like they had in the 1840s; their own world was bigger and more real than the world outside. It was as though a bell jar had been put over the town—and with the inn we did not want to let too much air in."

Thus Woollen Associates' design for the inn, because of its effort to be particular to New Harmony, stands in contrast to its designs for other projects, like the Pilot Center in Cincinnati or the Indiana University Arts Center. Some will also note that it stands in contrast to Philip Johnson's famous "roofless church," which is virtually next door to the inn and which can be seen in the lower left hand corner of the aerial photograph which precedes the text on page 40. (Reports indicate that the unfortunate deterioration of the church's ten-foot wall, and its consequent reduction in height by about half, have resulted in a happier scale relationship between it and the rest of the town.)

The New Harmony Inn consists of two separate buildings. The smaller one, and the one nearest the street, is the entry house, and it contains a registration area, a lobby and a small chapel in the rear. The lobby, which is shown

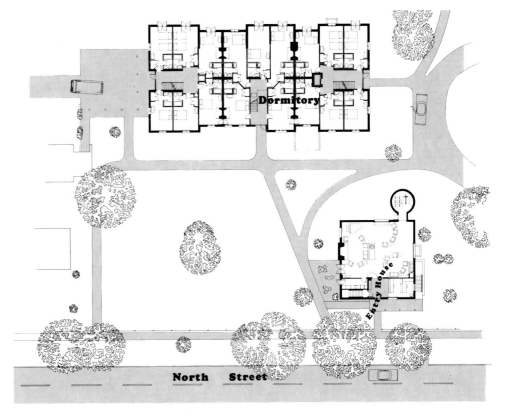

in the photograph above, is large enough to encourage meetings, lectures and small concerts; chairs, which are stored on the balcony level, can quickly be brought in for these purposes.

The larger building—or "dormitory" in allegiance to the lore of New Harmony—is organized not along long corridors, but according to the entry system, with rooms opening directly onto one of three stairways. There are double-height suites on the third floor of the inn, with sleeping lofts connected to the living levels by spiral stairs.

Woollen Associates' design for the New Harmony Inn seems in every way "situational"

—responsive to the context and the traditions of the place where it is built. But that raises a very important question: in being so modest, so particular to the place, is it being particular to *itself* (presuming, as architects usually do, that buildings are each meant in some way to be quite special)? Certainly no one would argue with the basic good sense of Woollen Associates' approach. But it is easy to wonder whether their example will or should be followed by other talented professionals who will assist in New Harmony's current rejuvenation. (Certainly New York architect Richard Meier, who was subsequently commissioned to design

a new visitors' center, did not choose to follow suit.) Whether the "situational" approach here satisfies everyone's expectations of what architecture should finally be, it seems eminently worth pointing out that that is certainly where it well must begin.

NEW HARMONY INN, New Harmony, Indiana. Architects: *Woollen Associates.* Engineers: *Robert Crooks* (structural); *D. A. Boyd Company* (mechanical and electrical). Consultant: *Kane and Carruth* (landscape). General contractor: *Chris Nix Company.*

THE REGENT OF FIJI
FIJI ISLANDS
Black O'Dowd
& Associates

The islands of Fiji lie at about 18 degrees south latitude on a line between the east coast of Australia and American Samoa. New Zealand is almost due south, and the preponderance of tourists to Fiji are vacationers from Down Under. They come mostly on packaged tours with a choice of several hotels. The most recent of these is the Regent Fiji Hotel, a 300-room facility designed by Black, O'Dowd and Associates of Palos Verdes, California.

The site is about 25 acres of land owned by a Fiji tribe that shares in development revenues. The architects designed eight residential buildings of 36 units each, eleven "bures"—deluxe suites in a Polynesian idiom—and a central structure housing kitchen, dining, shops, convention rooms and

hotel administration. Most are oriented to ocean views and respect the custom that no building may be taller than a coconut tree.

The living units are constructed chiefly in prefabricated and poured concrete with some construction timber coming from the U.S. and Canada. Exotic woods, local to this part of the Pacific, found many decorative uses. Most of the finishes are simple and durable; tile taking the place of carpet wherever practical in this moist climate.

The benign climate, of course, encourages the development of outdoor spaces and the architects have had fun with balconies, dining verandahs, and a host of outdoor activity spaces. All are developed and detailed with restraint and with a sensitive respect for local conditions. From every point

Wayne Thom photos

of vantage, the hotel presses lightly on the land and that is an attitude toward design as much as it is a construction reality. Almost anywhere this attitude appears it is welcome. In Fiji, for so long beyond the reach of most vacationers, it is especially welcome now that new air routes and schedules are beginning to open even the vast reaches of the central and South Pacific to tourism and development.

THE REGENT OF FIJI, Fiji Islands. Architects: *Black O'Dowd and Associates*. Associate architects: *Larson, Holtom, Maybin & Co.* Engineers: *Socoloske, Zelner & Associates* (structural); *Ambrose Engineering* (mechanical); *Daniel Laidman Associates* (elect) Interiors/Graphics: *William L. Pereira Assoc.* landscape: *EDAW;* contractor: *Fouche Construction.*

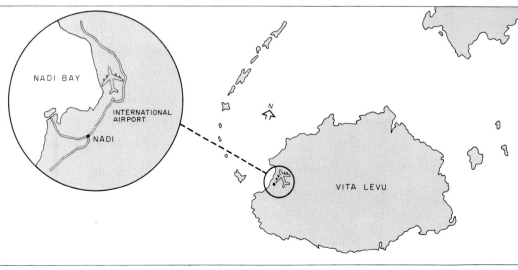

Julius Shulman photos

OJAI VALLEY INN, OJAI, CALIFORNIA
Peter L. Gluck & Associates

The photo above is of the lawn outside the original building of the Ojai Valley Inn, a romantic sort-of-Spanish-colonial building, located out of view to the right, and seen in the section, far right. That lawn, open to its splendid southern California views, is also the roof of the first phase of a 175-room addition to the Inn, let into the hillside below. The new building preserves the view, and exists where no new construction had been thought desirable—or even possible on its specific site. The partially hidden location also accomplishes something else: a building that can be both a straightforward modern statement and considerate of its romantic surroundings—including the adjacent town of Ojai. (As seen in the photo at left,

the town was carefully nurtured to its current well-protected and picturesque guise by developer Edward Liddy back in the 1920s.) But the new addition is not just interesting for its consideration. It also has an interesting structure that is—thanks to engineers Spiegel & Zamecnik—both innovative and economical enough to make the project possible in the first place.

The complete addition of 175 rooms is to be built in two stages, and the current construction is shown in the left half of the plan. The rooms are stepped down the side of the hill so that each room has spectacular views and a terrace partially sheltered by wood trellises. Access to the new rooms is from "corridors" against the retaining walls at each level (to the right in the section). These passages are designed for transportation directly to the doors of rooms by golf carts, and this mode of access overcomes any walking-distance problems that might arise from the plan's extreme linearity. Frequent light wells avoid any sense of being in a tunnel.

Gluck's successful intentions have produced a building that is both a straightforward contemporary design (or—as the architect states—"hard edge") and considerate of its romantic environment. And the result is to be softened even more than by its discreet placement. The stuccoed plywood walls are topped by a series of planters at each floor level. These produce a camouflage of vegetation that spreads over wire nets and the wood trellises above the decks outside of each room. Eventually, the construction will be perceived not as a new building, but as a series of new spaces.

The versatility of the architects' efforts to respect context is displayed by an entirely separate structure, a new gatehouse at the hotel entrance. This takes the form of a pierced wall with a cornice, and this wall conceals a functional gatehouse, which stands free behind it. Accompanied by an industrial-type lighting fixture on a stand, this composition is an exercise in historical recall, and forms an interesting contrast to the straightforward hotel addition.

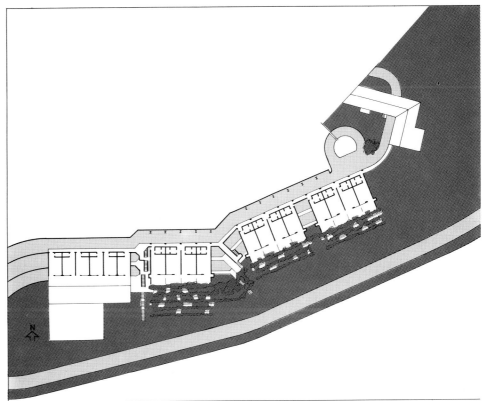

Planter boxes extend across the length of each floor, and also beyond the building in a series of bridges built with plywood box beams (photo above left). As visualized by the architects in the section below, growth from the planters is intended to form an eventual camouflage over the entire building, and to contain the outdoor spaces.

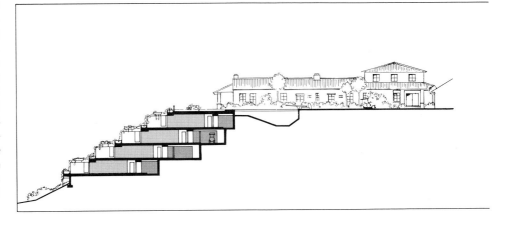

Because the building is set into a hillside in a series of stepped floors, and because the area is particularly subject to earthquakes, the feasibility of the project might have been in severe question if standard (and more expensive) structural techniques were used. The problem was accentuated by the single-loaded corridors and by the weight of 18 inches of earth on the uppermost roof.

Working with engineers Spiegel & Zamecnik, Gluck developed a composite system of plywood, steel and concrete—all of which work together to obtain the required rigidity at considerable cost savings over more normal construction. As explained in the diagram overleaf, both the horizontal forces of wind and possible earthquake are resisted in the direction perpendicular to the hill by plywood and wood-stud shear walls between each room. These walls are given rigidity by careful attention to nailed connections between the wood members and by two-inch-square steel tubes which connect the walls where they overlap (see section opposite and bottom detail at right) to the steel and concrete structure of the golf-cart passages nearest the hill.

Horizontal forces parallel with the hill are primarily resisted by the reinforced-masonry walls against the hill, to which the forces are transmitted by plywood and wood joist floor diaphragms. Rotation is resisted by the shear walls. Buttresses (as shown in the section) provide stability for the retaining walls against earth forces above and below.

OJAI VALLEY INN, Ojai, California. Owner: *Ojai Hotel Company*. Architects: *Peter L. Gluck and Associates—project team: Timothy Wood and Geoffrey Koper (job captain)*. Structural engineers: *Spiegel & Zamecnik Consulting Engineers*. Lighting consultant: *Sylvan R. Shemitz & Associates*. General contractor: *Macleod Construction Company*.

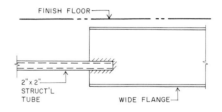

DETAIL **A**

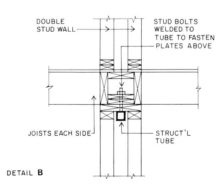

DETAIL **B**

The walls on the exposed part of the building are plywood diaphragms sheathed in stucco. The architects cite, as part of the substantial savings, the surprisingly light weight of timber and plywood that would—with proper care with connections—support required resistances to strong seismic forces. Structural details of the composite system are shown opposite and explain various parts of the section on this page and the diagrams overleaf. Twenty-inch-deep timber trusses supported by the stud walls carry the weight of the soil required for the lawn on the roof.

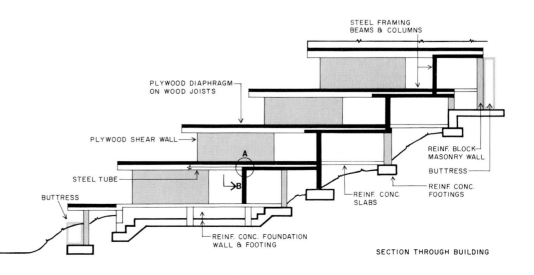

STEEL FRAMING BEAMS & COLUMNS

PLYWOOD DIAPHRAGM ON WOOD JOISTS

PLYWOOD SHEAR WALL

STEEL TUBE

BUTTRESS

REINF. BLOCK MASONRY WALL

BUTTRESS

REINF. CONC. FOOTINGS

REINF. CONC. SLABS

REINF. CONC. FOUNDATION WALL & FOOTING

A

B

SECTION THROUGH BUILDING

MISSISSIPPI QUEEN STEAMBOAT
Albert P. Hinckley, Jr.

William Muster

William Muster

This sternwheeler riverboat, berthed in Cincinnati, is a floating luxury hotel which made its maiden voyage in 1976. By the time this huge vessel (longer than a football field) left the pier, the construction costs had reached over $23 million. The Queen features seven decks, 218 staterooms, a swimming pool, sauna, movie theater, a two-deck dining room and a grand salon. It was conceived in the tradition of the great riverboats and was built to the stringent conditions of the U.S. Coast Guard.

The preliminary design was done by Albert P. Hinckley, Jr. the project architect, who then turned it over to a firm of naval architects and engineers for the structural and mechanical development while he assembled his design team. The designers, including architect David Beer of Welton Becket & Associates who was in charge of the interiors, agreed that the ship should be designed to exploit the limitations of modern passenger ship construction; use a limited range of colors, materials and forms; and be well detailed and executed. It was to be comfortable to live on, sumptuous and quiet in its public areas with lots of brass, bright stainless steel and potted palms. A beige and brown color palette was chosen, accented by red in the cinema and green in the entrance lounge. Since the bulkheads of the ship are heavily fenestrated, the designers decided that decorative effects should be largely confined to the ceilings. These consist of asbestos-composition panels four feet wide with eight-inch gaps. Over one hundred different designs have been silk screened to these panels.

From the exterior the steamboat is in the spirit of its great predecessors, including the Delta Queen. The proportions and details are correct and there is even a calliope on the top deck. In the tradition of riverboat design, the architects put the principal public rooms on a high deck to give the passengers an unobstructed view of the passing river scene. This arrangement also made it possible to give these rooms high ceilings. (In the old ships the saloon extended the full length of the vessel with clerestory windows over the flanking rows of cabins). On the Mississippi Queen, the cabins are on the three decks below the public rooms. All have private baths and many have private verandas. The passenger decks topside have a swimming pool, a sheltered bar and a sauna. The bottom deck contains crew accommodation, storage, boiler and engine rooms.

The tonnage of the Mississippi Queen is 3500, it is 379 feet long, with a 67 foot beam, an 8 foot draft and a clear height from the water line of 52 feet. It carries 385 passengers and a crew of 125. The calliope, said to be the largest in existence, can be seen in the photo above, just beyond the flag. The social center of the boat is the observation deck which contains the Grand Saloon and the Dining Saloon (opposite page top and bottom).

MISSISSIPPI QUEEN STEAMBOAT. Owner: *Delta Queen Steamboat Company.* Project architect: *Albert P. Hinckley, Jr.* Exterior designer: *James Gardner.* Interior designers: *Welton Becket & Associates—architect-in-charge: David Beer.* Project director: *James S. Demetrion.* Naval architects and marine engineers: *Three Quays Marine Services.* Applied designs: *Joyce Conwy-Evans, Des RCA.* Other designers: *Desmond Freeman* (mosaic floor); *Patricia Turner* (mermaids); *Phillip Kemp* (plaster bas reliefs of river boats); *Harry Gitlin* (lighting). Builder: *Jeffboat, Inc.*

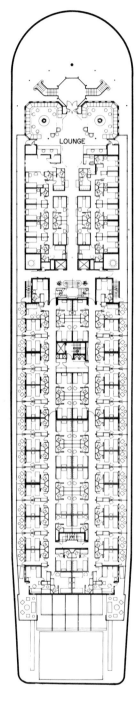

Marvin Rand photos, except as noted

The observation deck plan is shown at the left and the cabin deck plan at the right above. The port gallery (top left) has sleek contemporary furniture in effective contrast with the nostalgic silk-screened ornament on the asbestos-composition ceiling panels. The octagonal gazebo (bottom left) can be seen in the plan at the forward end of the observation deck. It is cheerfully Victorian in its carpet, stained glass and lattices. The grand stair, an essential element in all passenger ships which aspire to elegance, is very grand indeed on the Mississippi Queen (opposite page). The basic elements of David Beer's interior design scheme are all to be found here—the mirrors, the bright metals and the panels stencilled with Victorian ornament.

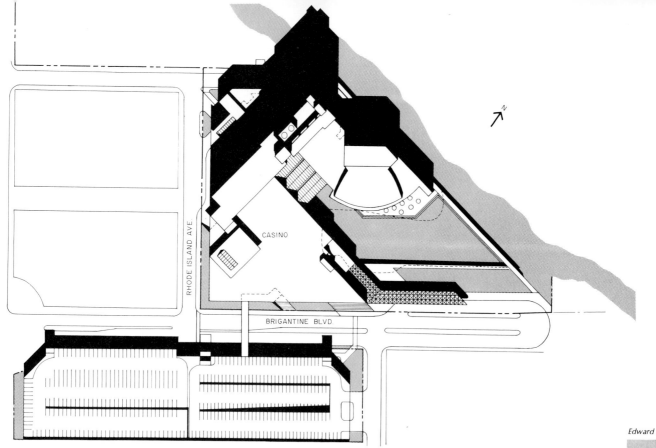

Edward Jacoby/APG photos

HARRAH'S MARINA HOTEL CASINO ATLANTIC CITY, NEW JERSEY
BWB Associates

It is the daily influx of gaming-bent high rollers and housewives from the populous Eastern corridor that most decisively shaped this new casino-hotel complex on the outskirts of Atlantic City. For while the hotel itself is of only moderate size (506 guest rooms), its normal complement of public spaces is vastly swollen by the need to accommodate, along with hotel guests, transients attracted by a casino with a capacity of 6,300 patrons.

The owner, Holiday Inns, through its recently acquired subsidiary, Harrah's, perceived the venture not only as its first foray into the lucrative gaming industry but as an opportunity to project a new and upscale image for a chain of hostelries hitherto best known for no-frills lodgings.

However, if the introduction to the complex of public amenities on a grand scale was prompted in part by the desire to tap a broader market, it was strongly encouraged by New Jersey's stringent regulations hedging

casino development. In a perhaps wistful effort to prevent gaming from becoming the only game in town, state and local agencies require that Atlantic City casinos be developed in conjunction with hotel space (in a ratio geared to casino area) and with other facilities deemed to constitute assets to the community as a whole. In consequence, despite the undeniable dominance of its 46,000-square-foot casino, Harrah's is also a full-fledged seaside resort and convention complex boasting—in addition to the hotel— a gamut of ancillary spaces ranging from conference and meeting rooms to a Broadway-size theater, from restaurants and bars to a "fun" center for children and teens.

Program dictates apart, the principal design determinant for architects BWB Associates was the site, previously untouched marshland on the shore of Absecon Bay a mile and a half north of Atlantic City. Although the structure appears on approach

to rise from the flats in splendid isolation, its site was in fact both cramped in size and difficult in configuration. Roughly pie shaped, it is hemmed on the south and west by the right-angle wedge formed by intersecting streets and on its northeast rim by an irregular shoreline penetrated by a tidal lagoon.

In spite—or because—of the site constraints relative to the sheer bulk of building volume required, the massing of the structure, says project designer Brian Thomson, "almost fell into place." The available land area is wholly blanketed by a three-story base building that houses the casino, all public spaces, and concomitant "back-of-the-house" facilities. The triangular casino, with administrative areas and meeting rooms on two levels above, occupies the apex of the wedge, its 500-foot-long hypotenuse defining the building's principal circulation spine. The curved peninsula between inlet and bayshore neatly embraces the sculpted arc of the thea-

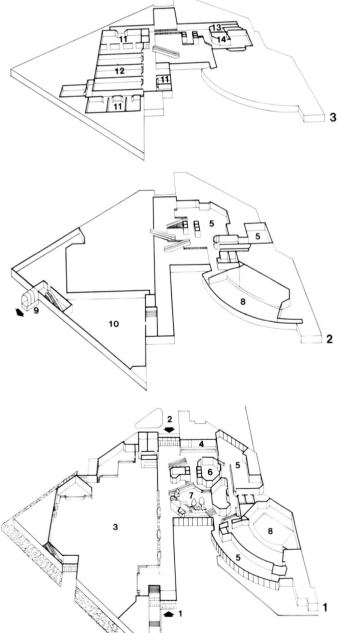

1   Casino entrance
2   Hotel entrance
3   Casino
4   Front desk
5   Restaurant
6   Shops
7   Atrium
8   Show theater
9   Bridge to garage
10 Administration/offices
11 Meeting rooms
12 Convention center
13 Hair salon
14 Recreation center

ter, with terraced snack bar below. And the two elements are linked by three levels of lounges, restaurants, and shops, all open to a skylit atrium lounge.

Surmounting the base building is the 12-story hotel tower, which is set perpendicular to the main circulation path through the building—an orientation that also optimizes views from the guestrooms. A 2,400-car garage is shoehorned onto a narrow plot across the street from the casino complex and connected to it by a second-level walkway.

From the outset, the tidal inlet was recognized to be a major design asset, offering the opportunity to strengthen the visual link between the complex and its coastal surround. The problem was to extend the lagoon inward to the building line—and to jump a 10-foot gap between its natural level and building grade—without upsetting the ecological balance of the tidal area and adjacent wetlands. The solution: a dam that contains the lagoon to its high-water level, and above it a pool that laps the building walls at

grade. Fresh water from the pool cascades to a trough atop the dam, from which it is recirculated, creating the illusion of a natural transition but preventing actual spillover of fresh water to the salt water inlet.

The expansive atmosphere generated by the exterior's space-framed arcade, boardwalks, lagoon and pool is carried through to interiors whose dominant theme might be summed by the designers' observation that "Atlantic City is not Las Vegas."

A central concern shared by the architects and by the interior design team, fielded by Hugh Stubbins and Associates, was to help the visitor orient himself in relation both to the potentially bewildering maze of functions and spaces within the building and to the outside environment. This aim was achieved by establishing straightforward and well-defined paths of circulation, which themselves have proved to be among the most successful of the building's spaces.

The dominant path is the broad main concourse that, rising the full three-story

height of the base building, cuts a diagonal swath through the complex from the modestly ceremonial casino entrance to the hotel entrance opposite. For most of its length it is open on one side to the glittering cavern of the casino. On the other side it traces the line of the lagoon, then expands to merge with the soaring volume of the glass-enclosed atrium and the three layers of lobbies, lounges, and other public spaces beyond. Open to concourse and atrium, these "balcony" areas form both a vertical circulation core and confirming points of orientation.

In keeping with the designers' desire to create an ambiance of warmth as well as festivity, the interiors are executed primarily in natural materials and contemporary idiom, notably free of pastiche. Gaiety and glitter—even glamour in some spaces—abound, but the prevailing spirit is perhaps best exemplified by the atrium lounge. Here wicker furniture, lavish plantings, and, above all, the uncluttered outlook to sky and sea join in a gracious bow to the Atlantic City of old.

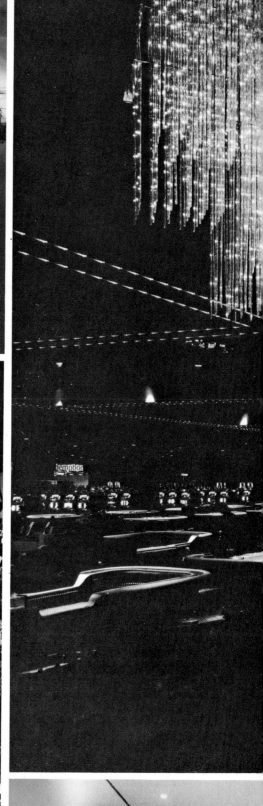

Inevitably, the centerpiece of Harrah's is its vast casino—a yawning cave of billiard-table green accented with every shade of neon, pooled with light and shadow, sparked with glitter. Because its floor is dense with gaming areas (and gamers), the designers put the ceiling to work as the principal locus of directional cues. The central corridor is brilliantly marked by chandeliers composed of acrylic tubes threaded with minilights whose twinkle also outlines the dropped beams used to organize the otherwise amorphous space. Overhead mirrors lend a festive—and practical—touch: they are one-way glass employed for surveillance.

The restaurants too gave the designers full scope to create "special" spaces, each in a style compatible with the type of menu and service offered. At the top of the line is an intimate "haute" restaurant overlooking the ocean and evoking its sense of low-key luxury through the use of muted colors and rich materials—linen and velvet, mahogany and brass. In striking contrast is the poolside snack bar, with its colorful but sturdy fittings and its lavish but functional rainbow banner ceiling.

HARRAH'S MARINA HOTEL CASINO, Atlantic City, New Jersey. Owner: *Harrah's, a subsidiary of Holiday Inns—Don Hart, director of casino development.* Architects: *BWB Associates—Claude Braganza, principal-in-charge; William Huntington, project manager; Brian Thomson, project designer; Don Pique, job captain.* Interior designers: *Hugh Stubbins and Associates, Inc.—Philip Seibert, director of interior design; Peter Scott, project manager; Molly Bunker, John Kelsey, Kathleen Rogers and Jean Veigas, designers; Erwin Winkler, artwork selection.* Consultants: *Daly & Daly (specialty signage); Redhouse Associates (exterior signage); Tom Pappas, Inc. (structural); GAI Associates, Inc. and Robert F. Sigel, Inc. (electrical); Gillium Brady Associates, Inc. (mechanical); Robert E. Hughey (environmental planning).* Construction management: *Perini Corp.*

While good design elsewhere may reflect reality, good design for restaurants often reflects the fantasy of escape. This is not to say that the premises will be cluttered with plastic paneling, plastic plants and three-dimensional wallpaper depicting far away places—all of which tend to be convincing only after several martinis. There can be a comforting atmosphere of being "away from it all" within the parameters of good design. And this atmosphere can be produced in any number of valid ways. These include the careful development of a theme that may have little to do with the immediate surroundings—especially when they are warehouses or office buildings. On the following pages, both the Backstreet Restaurant by Mark Simon, of Moore Grover Harper, and the Whole Grain by Wudtke Watson Davis are successful examples of the latter approach. Another restaurant, Levana's by Rodolfo Imas, evokes a theme, but the theme is an abstraction of New York City, where it is located.

Whatever the approach, the design of the successful full-service restaurant will accomplish certain goals. It will produce that seductive environment for the relaxed experience of dining, instead of simply eating and drinking in public. (Oversimplified, the lighting will not be too high nor the decor too intrusive.) It will also set a stage for watching other people, a strong motive in going out. (There might be a center of attention, perhaps a flight of stairs, somewhere near the entrance.) And it will convey a message about the food and the clientele. Of course, the biggest psychological factor in having a successful restaurant, besides good food, is to have the place full of people. And this should happen as a result of meeting the design goals.

It may be most instructive to observe those restaurants on the following pages which meet successful design goals without a superimposed theme. The Ciao Ristorante by Ron Nunn Associates is a straightforward storefront restaurant with simple furniture and a tile floor. Its very simplicity evokes the best of modern Italian design, and gives a strong clue, as does the restaurant's name, to the fare that will be offered on the menu. Both the Millcroft Inn by Hamilton Ridgely Bennett and the Bear Mountain Inn by Joseph Tonetti & Associates are rugged direct expressions of the kinds of buildings that they are in. They capitalize on the inherent drama of fine old buildings. Windows on the World by Warren Platner Associates is designed for dining with a spectacular view, and—if it has a theme—that theme can be most accurately called luxury itself. The lavish materials and detailing enhance a feeling of well being high in the clouds.

And so it can be seen that each architect has tackled the problems of restaurant design in ways that reflect the particular circumstances of location, type of restaurant, client's desires and architect's point of view. After such standard problems as air conditioning, kitchen service and accommodating the desired number of seats have been solved, a process has taken place that achieves a unique and particularly appropriate result. Each project offers that very important attribute of a restaurant: the patron feels he or she is somewhere special.

Chapter Three

Restaurants and Lounges

CIAO RISTORANTE SAN FRANCISCO, CALIFORNIA
Ron Nunn Associates

Through plate-glass windows, San Francisco's new Ciao Ristorante sends an unmistakable message to passers-by on the sidewalk: warmth, light, talk, food—all the inimitable qualities of friendly Italian *trattorias*, where customers not only enjoy their meals but enjoy being seen enjoying.

Inside, the food part of the message is equally clear. At one end of the bar, chefs mix, shape and boil pasta in a large display area, where pots of sauce and other dishes are prepared within sight and smell of diners seated on terraces around the room or at the marble-topped bar. Counters in the display area also have surfaces of marble, the material preferred by cooks mixing and handling dough. The kitchen itself is used chiefly for broiling and dishwashing.

Architect Ron Nunn believes that "people are tired of being tucked away in dark places" when they eat out. But creating a bright restaurant in this case required the transformation of a fashionably Stygian disco that earlier occupied these quarters in an old brick commercial building on historic Jackson Square.

The primary step was to strip the wall of black paint and to replace the black ceiling. The wood planking thus revealed has been painted off-white, and matches the new rubber-tile flooring that replaced dark gray carpet. The textured surface of the planked wall and the glint of brass railings add visual warmth and light to the bright decor, as do mirrors—left over from the disco—on walls and columns. White enameled industrial lighting fixtures hang over each table.

Ciao's owners, who operate other restaurants in the city, see this as a prototype for similar establishments.

CIAO RISTORANTE, San Francisco, California. Owners: *Larry Mindel and Jerry Magnin, principals in Spectrum Foods, Inc.* Architects: *Ron Nunn Associates.* Contractor: *Filer Brothers Corp.*

Russell Abraham photos

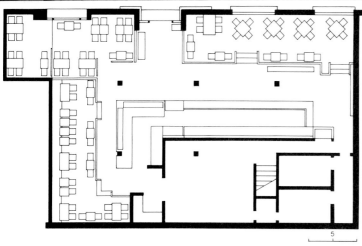

BACKSTREET RESTAURANT NEW HAVEN, CONNECTICUT
Mark Simon, Moore Grover Harper

Eclecticism isn't what it used to be. No longer does the architect combine one delicate detail with another, ever so delicately. Rather he gulps both general form and delicate details, and then, like an architect, synthesizes the whole conglomeration. And if he's good at it, he will produce a feast for the eyes and *bon mots* for the knowing.

At the Backstreet Restaurant in New Haven, Connecticut, architect Mark Simon has used neon tubing both for lighting and as a source for form. The pink and orange neon around the bar is operated by a dimmer—a bit of wizardry—so that it emits a more seductive glow than normally intense neon, "like candlelight without the flicker." Tubes behind the mirror shine through clear glass where silver backing has been removed. The neon light is reflected in the bar and into the dining room by shiny pressed tin panels hung from the ceiling, in reference both to Victorian saloons and to the radiant coronas that Baroque sculptors hung above statues.

Moreover, the bar itself, the counter behind it and the neon lights conform in shape, the fat cylindrical railing recalling the lighted tubes, the bulbous corners resembling the curves taken when the glass tubes are melted and shaped.

The owners envisioned Backstreet as a visual "explosion" to excite customers at lunch, dinner and evening jazz sessions. At the same time, Simon feels that dining facilities should be "comfortable," and so gave the restaurateurs what he calls "carefully considered excess." The burst of visual impressions is tempered by soothing pastels.

BACKSTREET RESTAURANT, New Haven, Connecticut. Owners: *Larry Oranzo and Steven Kuziel.* Architects: *Mark Simon of Moore Grover Harper, PC—Frank Cheney, project manager.* Engineer: *Fred Broberg* (electrical). Consultants: *Lucien Addario* (plants and flowers); *Catherine Ferucci* (graphics). Contractors: *Gus Dudley, Donald Langella* (general); *Arc Electric, Signlite and Jo-Ran Neon* (electrical); *Breakfast Woodworks (Louis Mackall and Kenneth Field).*

Norman McGrath photos

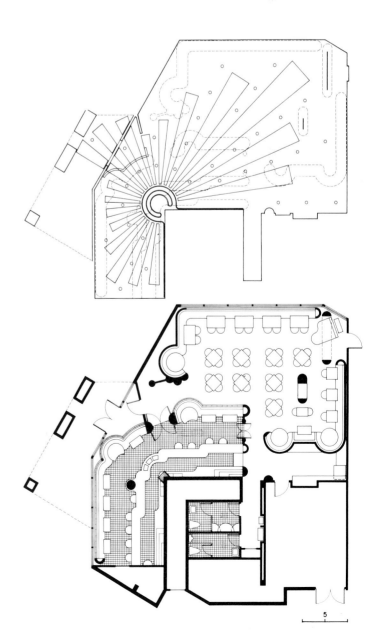

5

LEVANA'S
NEW YORK CITY
Rodolfo Imas

Norman McGrath photos

Depending on the season and/or the hour, Levana's presents either a cold grid facade to 67th Street or a highly variegated, highly punctured, and more inviting face.

Diners at Levana's Bakery on West 67th Street in Manhattan would be surprised to hear that they are sitting in a restaurant with New York City as its stated theme—there's not so much as a passing reference to the Empire State Building or the Statue of Liberty. Though architect Rodolfo Imas intended to capture and recall the spirit of Manhattan in Levana's, he rendered the motif abstract rather than literal, oblique rather than direct—opting for ambiance over caricature.

Four years after leaving Buenos Aires to establish a practice in New York, Imas makes his U.S. architectural debut with Levana's. The commission was provided by his accountant, who, along with two brothers, owned a kosher carry-out bakery: when the twin space adjacent to the bakery became available, the brothers decided to expand their operation and include table service.

Despite the addition of a restaurant, the clients wanted to maintain their carry-out business; staggered shifts for each operation suggested a clear separation of the two. Imas pushed the tables to the rear, creating a single-access cruciform enclosure (axonometric overleaf); dropped the ceiling to create a more intimate scale and add definition; and inserted an oak floor to further articulate the dining area. The sales area was placed along the transparent street facade to ensure maximum visibility of the baked goods, and for minimal intrusion upon the restaurant: the black rubber flooring is a response to the heavier flow of customer traffic. In addition to providing a display window, the formidable grid facade (infilled with wire glass) can be re-adjusted to transform Levana's from an enclosed interior bakery/restaurant to an open-air cafe: two massive doors swing open and a pair of steps pull down for seating (photo middle right). Even when closed the facade is engaging: visual syncopation is provided by three red columns and a transverse beam that frame the heavy grid. While Imas credits the facade for providing an appropriate "architectonic and urban presence," it also—owing to the strength of the steel—functions as a night security gate.

The theme of grid-as-urban-symbol is reiterated and carried to the interior by means of a cage-like structure that serves as counter and display case for the bakery (photo far right); above the sales area, a series of cubes ascend and graduate toward the ceil-ing—according to Imas, "to integrate the urban environment into the space." Though the idea is abstract, the contrast between the cold steel grid—in all of its permutations—and warm wood benches, pastel pink/peach walls, and dramatic lighting is striking.

Imas felt that his scheme for the expansion should take its design cues from the city and the raw space. As a newcomer to Manhattan, the Argentinian architect was impressed with what he refers to as the "New York urban folklore." Though seasoned New Yorkers may consider brownstone stoops, Central Park benches, and subway grating the everyday facts of urban life, Imas identifies each of these elements as specific referents given expression in his design: they are collectively, the motif by which Levana's achieves its New York City-theme-restaurant status. And though the source list is arbitrary, and the architectural execution highly personal, the resultant design does, if only figuratively, convey the urbane character of Manhattan, while acknowledging the structural fact of two distinct spaces now combined to make one. Imas draws parallels between the massive grid facade and a subway grating, between the wooden benches and Central Park seating, and between the steps pulling out from the facade and a brownstone stoop: considerably less arcane is the brash red line signaling structure, both present (columns and beams) and past (where the former wall once stood dividing the bakery from its neighboring retail shop). And to remind diners that "the structure belongs to the building, not to the restaurant," Imas outlined the transverse beams with narrow strips of mirror—creating the illusion of a section cut through the building.

Although most customers will not find meaning in all the abstract and symbolic gestures Imas employed to provide Levana's with its urbane character, it is, according to the owners, a rare customer who doesn't notice and applaud the design. The owners add—not incidentally—that, since the bakery's re-opening, business is better than ever, and the restaurant is flourishing.

LEVANA'S, New York, New York. Owners: *Avram, Maurice, and Sol Kirschenbaum.* Architect: *Rodolfo Imas—Amalka Cobdra, Ricardo Prieto* (production assistants). Contractors: *Azzo Constructions (general); Artistic Metal Work (storefront).*

By choosing a cruciform plan for the restaurant—reinforced by the track lighting, and by the intersection of transverse and longitudinal beams—Imas effectively isolated the table-service area from the bakery: the seating plan also provides every table with a corner. The benches and tables are transparent, making the diminutive space seem larger. Take-out service is facilitated by being placed between the two oversized doors—customers can enter and exit unobtrusively.

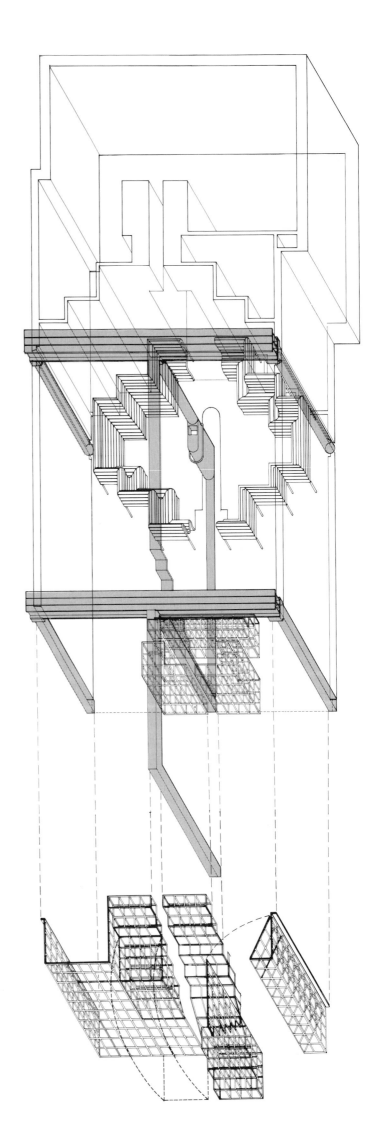

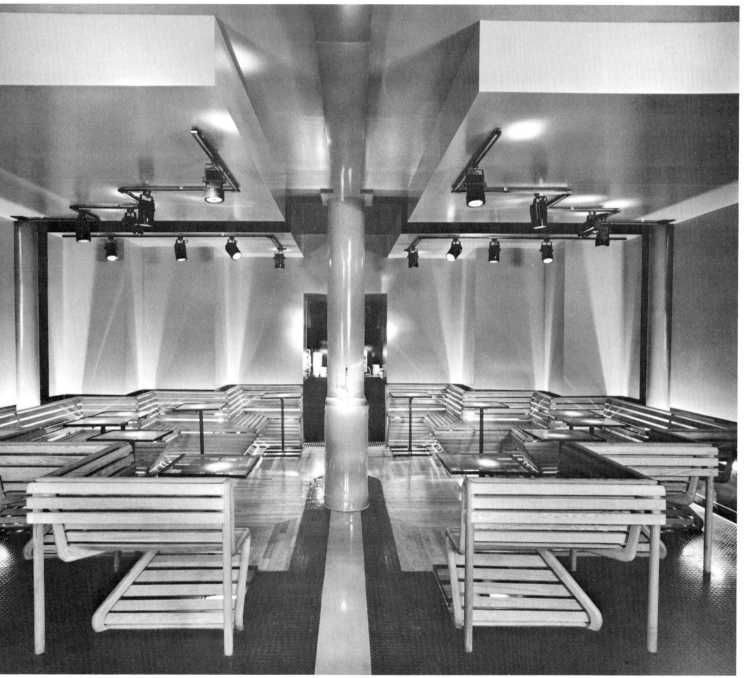

A brilliant red line cuts through the center of the kosher restaurant to signal an erstwhile wall that once divided Levana's from an adjacent retail shop: the gesture is repeated along the longitudinal beam to signal structure. A massive fountain was attached to the center column (photo top) to recognize and permit the Orthodox Jewish ritual of washing hands prior to eating.

In designing this restaurant in Cleveland, architects Wudtke Watson Davis have created a simple but theatrical environment where all eyes are on the appetizing displays. *And* they have created a particular imagery that tells in the presentation a lot about the food. The Whole Grain is the result of a program by client Stouffers to develop a prototype design that would bring older restaurants into line with both current ideas about simple, lighter foods, and about more self-service. (Here, the main business is lunch.) The architects were involved in everything from the prototype's name and the increased efficiency of the angled self-service counters, to the design of the kitchen. A basic design problem was the space on the ground floor of a highrise office building. It was the sort of leftover space that exists after higher rent facilities have been carved out on the desirable perimeter. An early decision was to program the remote area (bottom of plan) as a required take-out facility. In the main space, vertical existing obstructions were used to separate tables into more intimate groups—while still maintaining views toward the carefully arranged and lighted self-service counter. Due to the limited peak hours of operation, it was essential that as many diners be accomodated as possible without crowding, and this was accomplished by both a tight seating plan, separated by level changes for privacy, and by the use of high tables with stools in locations where low seats would have produced a feeling of being closed in.

THE WHOLE GRAIN, Cleveland, Ohio. Owner: *The Stouffer Corporation.* Architects: *Wudtke Watson Davis, Inc.—principal-in-charge: Donald E. Wudtke; design architect: Will Adams; project architect: Dan Whitney; interior designer: Kit Cameron.* Engineers: *William and Hack (structural); Denk-Kish Associates, Inc. (mechanical/electrical).* Consultants: *Robert Green Design (interiors/graphics); The Marshall Associates (food service).* General contractor: *Schirmer-Schneider.*

THE WHOLE GRAIN CLEVELAND, OHIO
Wudke Watson Davis

Dan Whitney photos

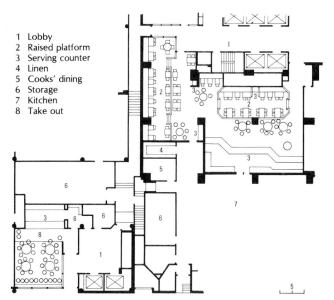

1 Lobby
2 Raised platform
3 Serving counter
4 Linen
5 Cooks' dining
6 Storage
7 Kitchen
8 Take out

THE MILLCROFT INN
ALTON, ONTARIO
Hamilton Ridgely Bennett

According to the jury's report accompanying a recent award from the Ontario Association of Architects: "The Millcroft Inn in Alton is an outstanding example of the thoroughness, involvement and integrity which architecture should represent." What the jury recognized was the way in which completely contemporary detailing—such as hardware, railings and light fixtures—had been carefully used to enhance, rather than disturb, the atmosphere of the building, built as a mill in 1881. Indeed, a second look reveals that much more than detailing is completely contemporary. For instance, the dining room, a large area, is divided by changes in floor level to achieve greater intimacy. The spaces thus created flow into each other in a very contemporary way, and are modulated by such devices as the overhead lattice-screen wall. Exposed stone walls and old wood decking on the ceiling here seem entirely appropriate, and capitalize on the pastoral waterside setting.

Corridors for access to twenty-two bedrooms on the upper floors surround a new skylighted well that brings natural light to the public rooms below. This whole approach to mixing the best of several eras is accomplished and noteworthy. The inn is part of a $2.5 million-dollar hotel complex on a 100-acre site.

THE MILLCROFT INN, Alton, Ontario, Canada. Architects: *Hamilton Ridgely Bennett—project architect: William Bennett; partner-in-charge-of-interiors: Gordon Ridgely.* Engineers: *Peter Sheffield & Associates* (structural); *Smith Andersen* (mechanical); *ECE Group* (electrical). Landscape architect: *Knecht & Berchtold.* Furniture services: *Elizabeth Geddes Designers Ltd.* General contractor: *E.G.M. Cape Construction Ltd.*

GROUND FLOOR

Applied Photography Ltd. photos

George Cserna photos

A freshly-cut skylight over the stairwell (left), and a sleek glass brick wall (far left and below) allow natural light to pour through the once-gloomy interior of the old Bear Mountain Inn. Cavernous eating areas were brightened with hanging industrial fixtures and zigzagging fluorescent strips in the cafeteria (far left), and by circular fixtures with miniature white bulbs in the formal dining room (below left).

The Old Bear Mountain Inn in the Ramapo Mountains of New York had been a landmark for more than three generations. Built in 1914 as a bus terminal and shelter for visitors, the inn had provided eating facilities for 60 years as the focal point of a popular resort that featured swimming, boating, skiing, hiking, and cultural events.

Though the inn's rustic exterior had retained its beautiful Alpine appearance over the years, the building's decaying interior had become a jumble of congested space and dark, gloomy eating areas. Architects Joseph Tonetti & Associates were faced with the task of preserving the inn's historic charm while upgrading dining facilities and lounge areas to handle increasing crowds of visitors to the state park.

Working on a state-allotted budget of approximately $2.1 million, the architects redesigned the building's entrances and exits, and gutted much of the existing interior in pursuit of their two major objectives—to provide better traffic circulation and to get more light into the musty, old inn.

"I enjoy renovation immensely," said architect Tonetti, of the challenge. "Working with an old building is like a puzzle. There are all sorts of things you have to work with and around, and solving the problems is like completing a puzzle."

A major problem was that the building had only one main entrance which opened into a tiny foyer housing the inn's narrow circular stairway. Other exits were rarely used and the main entrance was usually a bottleneck. The problem was solved by removing the circular stairway and creating a large, tiled entry foyer with adjoining hat check area in that space. The architects used a glass brick wall to conceal the downstairs cafeteria just off the foyer, and a wide new stairway to second floor dining and lounge areas was added beyond the foyer. A dramatic 15-by 20-foot skylight was then cut over the stairway to flood the dark center of the building with light.

All building exits and entrances were defined by using custom-made cream and brown awnings for a crisp but subdued effect that blended with the inn's turn-of-the-century flavor.

The only major addition to the inn's exterior was a concrete patio dining area off the inn's west side which was designed to conceal the loading area and garbage bins while offering visitors a tranquil view of Hessian Lake. The patio was furnished with

The only major addition to the inn's well-preserved exterior was a new concrete patio dining area, which conceals loading area and trash bins (left). Preservation was also the primary concern in the inn's main lounge (below). Layers of dirt and old varnish were stripped from the original chestnut ceiling and old chandeliers were repaired. Oak floor and furniture blend with the log-cabin air.

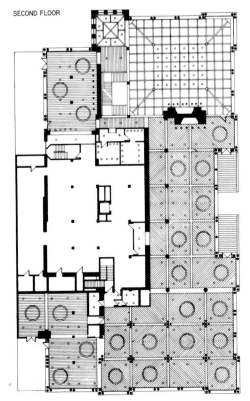

SECOND FLOOR

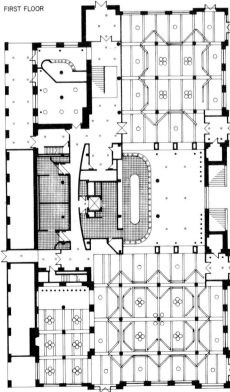

FIRST FLOOR

durable industrial stacking chairs and custom-made tables, with awnings that coordinated with those at entrances and exits.

In the main lounge and dining room on the second level, there was much that, despite decaying appearances, needed to be preserved. "Some of the old-timers were very apprehensive—they hated to see anything at all changed," said Tonetti.

Preserving the lounge's original chestnut ceiling, which was black with dirt and old varnish, the architects stripped and sealed the old wood, and installed unobtrusive linear diffusers for air supply. Quaint old chandeliers were also spruced up by replacing wood parts and cleaning lanterns. An unsightly temporary bar in the lounge was removed, and a handsome new oak bar was constructed in the corner created by moving the original stairwell. Custom-made oak lounge furniture was designed to echo the log-cabin style of the inn.

The old wood floors in the lounge and dining rooms, which were badly deteriorated, were replaced with Appalachian white oak, a material used throughout the inn's renovation for its light color.

In the dining room, drab acoustical tile ceilings were also redone in white oak and mirrored walls and cabinets were used to give the illusion of increased spaciousness and light. The old lighting fixtures in the dining room, which vaguely resembled yellowing parchment paper stretched over a wheel, were replaced by circular fixtures with tiny white bulbs, creating a star-like quality in the dining area at night.

The main dining room was furnished with oak tables that may be covered for formal dinners or used without tablecloths for breakfast and brunch. Caned bentwood chairs were used in the dining room while informal, low-backed oak chairs and bar stools were installed in the smaller Cub Room just off the lounge.

The major portion of the inn's renovation however, was done in the first floor cafeteria. Like the rest of the inn, it needed new plumbing, electrical and mechanical systems and its antiquated food service and storage facilities needed to be replaced. The dismal cafeteria had a low greying canvas ceiling that was hung with old Japanese lantern fixtures. The walls were covered with dark paneling and plaster, and the large eating area was cut into inefficient chunks of space by walls added in an earlier renovation.

The first floor was gutted to expose windows and old stone walls hidden behind dark paneling. A spacious new main entry foyer and stairwell (right, second to bottom) and auxiliary entrances and exits improved traffic circulation, providing more pleasant and efficient dining in the cafeteria (below and top right), the main dining room and the Cub Room (right, second to top).

In an effort to restore as much of the original building as possible, the architects gutted the first floor, exposing and restoring the inn's beautiful old stone walls and arches, and opening the arched windows to let light in. The glass brick wall, which complemented the texture of the stone walls, was used to separate the cafeteria from the foyer.

The old quarry tile floor, a gift of Robert Moses from the 1939-40 New York World's Fair, was still in good shape, and was simply cleaned, patched, and sealed with polyurethane.

Removing several layers of ceiling added in earlier renovations, the architects installed a new pressurized ceiling to increase air circulation while avoiding extensive duct work. The new ceiling was then finished with spray-on acoustical plaster following the structural contours.

Since the first floor cafeteria frequently had to function both as a fast food eating area and as a banquet hall, the new lighting and furniture had to do double duty. The eating areas were given hanging industrial incandescent fixtures for subdued banquet lighting and track lighting was used to wash the stone walls with soft light. Zig-zagging fluorescent strips were used to brighten the area for quick meals during the day.

In the cafeteria, Tonetti chose butcher block tables, and stacking chairs done in oak that lend a more formal look than the chairs used on the patio eating area. Sliding or folding oak doors that disappear into the walls were also installed to curtain off space, separating the enormous cafeteria and dining room into smaller banquet rooms.

Finally, the fast food service area in the cafeteria was enlarged and moved further out into the eating area, permitting more direct traffic circulation from the outside and increasing the efficiency of the service.

Graphics in the eating areas and throughout the lodge were designed to harmonize with furnishings and were later silk-screened and installed by the Park Service.

BEAR MOUNTAIN INN, Bear Mountain, New York. Owner: *The Palisades Interstate Park Commission.* Architect: *Joseph Tonetti & Associates—principal architect: Joseph Tonetti; project architect: Richard Jansen; designer: Rex P. Lalire.* Consultants: *Goldreich, Page & Thropp (structural engineering); Flack & Kurtz (mechanical and electrical engineering); Harry T. Skolodz (food service); The Wolf Company (cost).* Contractors: *Elite Construction Company (construction).*

Alexandre Georges photos

WINDOWS ON
THE WORLD/THE CLUB
NEW YORK CITY
Warren Platner Associates

From the moment a party arrives at *Windows,* the people are treated to a visual feast that in its way is as breathtaking as the view of the harbor and city spread out below. After an elevator trip that covers the 1300-foot vertical lift in 58 seconds, diners are received in a golden reception room (shown later), then enter a crystalline gallery (shown above) in which photo-murals of New York and great pieces of semi-precious stone from around the world are reflected and re-reflected from glass arches and mirrors on the walls, floor, and ceiling. In this space, images are so kaleidoscopic that for some the walk is like a trip through space; for others, a walk across a bridge defined only by the golden carpet. The gallery gradually widens, lighted at the far end by a luminous mass of color—which proves to be (when you arrive there) light from windows shining through the bottles stacked in the back bar. From there, is but a few steps down to tables along "The Windows" (photos above).

As the plan overleaf will show, virtually all of the perimeter space is given over to table space; and, conversely, no one dines without a view. But that is only the beginning step in

Platner's design concept of making each table—as nearly as possible—"the best seat in the house." People who come to Windows on the World "expect a special occasion; they expect a special place." Platner's skill in creating that "special place"—for each of 1000 diners—is evident in all of the photos; but perhaps best expressed in the photos above of the main dining room, which seats between 300 and 350.

The principle involved is a simple one: Create relatively small intimate spaces amidst what is, in fact, a very large area by changes in level and by enclosures that say "this space is special." To begin with, the main dining room—the largest open space—is divided into three spaces because it was positioned at the corner sharing the best night-time views uptown to the towers of New York, and to the east, overlooking the striking tracery of the lights on the East River bridges and the ship traffic on the river far below.

Throughout the spaces, further division is created by many changes of level. To give everyone a view, the tables are terraced up in steps away from the windows; and there are even changes of level within the terraces. (The given ceiling height is 12 feet.) Finally, as the photos show, there is a rich variety of dividing enclosures separating the tables, all in fine materials and carefully detailed. Typical of the thought given by Platner to make each seat that "best in the house": the narrow strip of mirror set into the back of each banquette gives every diner not facing a window an eye-level glimpse of the view, and also catches some of the light and glitter and movement in the room—reinforcing the luminous quality of the space and multiplying the images.

For all of the richness in detail and finishes, in plan Windows on the World is as carefully and functionally organized as an industrial plant. Upon arrival at the reception area, visitors, who are typically anxious to see the view, can take a moment to step up into the Statue of Liberty Lounge (arrow 1 in plan) which offers a spectacular panorama of New York Harbor. By raising the lounge close to the ceiling, Platner not only created a particularly mind-boggling downward view, but gave the small lounge a great sense of importance, created a strong vertical separation between

lounge and the south dining room some eight steps below (second photo from top, at right) and (more mundanely) created space beneath the lounge for a small dishwashing room which serves the separate grill kitchen.

Having had their first glimpse, visitors then move to their tables. Those attending a banquet move through a short hallway (arrow 2) to the West Parlor (photo next page). The Parlor, one of only two perimeter areas not given over to tables, serves as a reception area for the bank of banquet rooms, seating nearly 400 in total. The banquet rooms, with seating

for as few as six to eight or as many as 150, stretch along all of the west wall overlooking the Hudson River, and extend around the corners into the south and north walls.

Those to be seated in the grill or the main dining room have a longer walk—and Platner's plan not only makes that walk (arrow 3 on plan) an experience in itself, but minimizes any distraction or sense of bustle for those already at their place. Visitors walk through the beautiful glass gallery described earlier and pictured overleaf and in the photo top right. Those to be seated in the bar or grill turn right

82

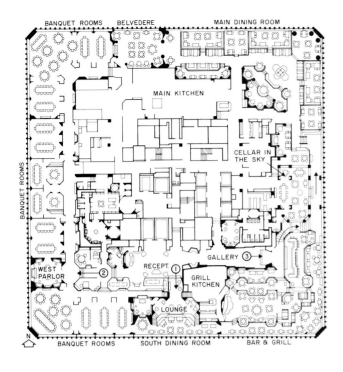

The Belvedere (opposite) is an elegant room, which can be used for private parties, opened to the banquet space (beyond the iris painting), or opened to the main dining room via the glass doors in the foreground. The special detailing includes the deeply sculptured ceiling, very private alcoves at the four corners, a general gold tone throughout that works well with the strong flat north light, and is accented by the gold leaf pattern on both sides of the entry door and the columns covered with gold-glazed and deeply arched ceramic tile.

The plan is described below.

at the end of the gallery, then move down banks of steps to the various terraced levels of that space at the southeast corner of the building. Those moving to the main dining room move left at the end of the gallery. Since it is, from that point, still a considerable walk to the dining room, Platner's plan offers the visitors another visual treat—a walk along the east windows with their view of the East River bridges far below.

That stretch of "window walk" creates the only interior dining space—the Cellar in the Sky—and it received a very special treatment

of its own (photos just above). Its entrance is announced with a flourish of brass handrails, which continues onto the gold leaf of the glass doors. Within, deeply arched ceilings frame glass walls, and those walls are lined with the supply of banquet wine in geometric wire racks. The "walls" of bottles offer glimpses of the spaces outside; and give the room an extraordinary light, supplemented by lighting designed to give the dappled effect visible in the photos.

Another "special place" is the Belvedere (photo opposite), described in the caption.

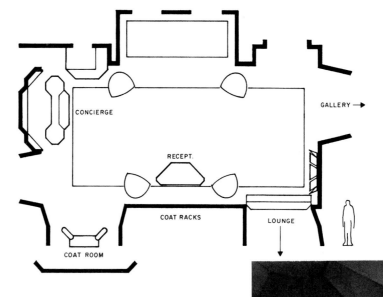

Careful detailing everywhere: At left, the West Parlor, which serves as a reception room for the banquet area. As everywhere, every element in the room from the rug to the lighting fixture was designed by the architect. Below left: a detail in the reception area, beginning the repetitive pattern of reflected and re-reflected images. Below: the concierge's desk and the reception table. At right, the men's room and the coat desk, designed to seem to provide the services of a personal valet. The highly mechanized coat racks are out of sight to each side. Opposite: the bar.

Part of the sense of "special occasion, special place" created at Windows on the World is the sense that everything received careful design attention. And it did. For example, the iris painting (previous spread) covers what, in fact, are quite handsome doors to the banquet rooms; but because it is a painting of flowers—symbol of hospitality—it creates a background for an elegant dining room; whereas doors visible at both ends of the room would have suggested that it was a passageway.

Other evidence of Platner's effort to make everything "special":

The photo at left shows the sculptured table which serves as a reception desk at noontime when the restaurant is a club; and simply as a decoration at night. It is backed by a gold-leafed wall, on which are gold globes strongly top-lighted. The pointillist pattern established here is repeated everywhere through the restaurant—in the carpet, in the tufting of much of the upholstery, in wool and silk tassels applied to the fabric in the dining alcoves. This consistent decorative element enriches all of the spaces without distracting from the essential architectural forms.

Another strong element: the pattern of the window wall at the Trade Center is of course pervasive—in a pattern of 27 inches of glass to 13 inches of solid wall. In such large spaces, this pattern read, to Platner's eye, "like a picket fence;" and so, at each column, he placed an ivory plastic-laminate half-tube, "creating the effect of an open colonnade without windows."

In the bar (photo above), Platner created another private world, set back from the windows but raised so that everyone shares the view.

This same design attention is evident everywhere. And the result is that Windows on the World is not just wonderful, but works.

WINDOWS ON THE WORLD and THE CLUB AT THE WORLD TRADE CENTER, North Tower, World Trade Center, New York City. Architects and designers: *Warren Platner Associates Architects—associates of Warren Platner on this project: Robert Brauer, Harvey Kaufman (project architect, design), Jesse Lyons (project architect, construction), Mark Morgaridge, Paul Sargent, Lee Ahlstrom, Gordon Black, Anita Holland-Moritz, Ron Grantham.* Consultants: *Cini-Grissom Associates (kitchen), Skilling Helle Christiansen Robertson (structural), Jaros Baum & Bolles (mechanical), Joseph Loring & Associates (electrical), Emery Roth & Son (building code), Vance Jonson (special graphics), Milton Glaser Inc. (menu graphics).* Owners: *Port Authority of New York and New Jersey.* Operators: *Inhilco, a subsidiary of Hilton International.* Project management: *Joseph Baum.* All art was conceived or designed by the architect. These artists collaborated in realization of the artwork: *Emily Elman, Ross Elmi, Panos Ghikas, Alexandre Georges, Vance Jonson, Susan Leites, Paul Linfante, Fred Werner, Haruo Miyauchi and, from Platner's office, Lee Ahlstrom, Gordon Black, Anita Holland-Moritz, and Harvey Kaufman.*

W
here once parks were places for such pleasurable pursuits as a quiet chat on a bench or a decorous stroll amidst the carefully controlled beauties of nature, they are often something quite different today. With changing lifestyles and the emergence of a general feeling that all public facilities should serve the broadest possible range of people, parks have been called upon to accommodate an amazing variety of recreational and even commercial pursuits — just as the increasing costs of maintenance have discouraged the parterres, topiary, exotic-plant species and other horticultural extravaganzas of the past. Urban parks offer a particular dilemma to current designers, because their previous less intensive use was far more compatible with an important urban goal: to create oases of greenery among the buildings. This need is felt more strongly today than ever. While woefully limited in area, parks are now under the most intense pressure to accommodate the active recreational and other outdoor pursuits of a community. Accommodating such conflicting aims is not easy.

For instance, the first project on the following pages, architects Bohlin Powell Brown Larkin Cywinski's Public Square in Wilkes-Barre, would have been a decorative set piece, a green punctuation in the city fabric, if conceived earlier in the century. There would have been a raised classical fountain centered on radiating paths among trees, and lots of flower beds. It is a tribute to the architects' skill that they maintained this valid decorative role in a new guise, while accommodating a weekly farmers market, civic ceremonies, festivals and theatrical performances. The inevitable bandstand has been replaced by a useful stage and the flowers by the less perishable ornament of molded brick.

Offering a different view into creatively transformed traditional values, architect Edward Larrabee Barnes has restored the Conservatory of the New York Botanical Garden. Conceived in the age of plentiful maintenance, this beautiful cast iron and glass confection exists today only because of the determination of the architect and of Enid Haupt (who donated the restoration monies) and because a program of educational uses justifies the high cost of maintaining the exotic flora within. Another park structure by Barnes, the administration and visitors center for the Chicago Horticultural Society, is a modern-day equivalent of the conservatory that combines greenhouses with even more practical functions.

Typical of the kind of parks that are being built today, Cincinnati's Forum by architects Louis Sauer Associates is a lively mix of fountains and theater that is designed to fulfill an urban-planning function: the tying together of several sections of a new waterfront development. All of these projects make a strong contribution to the art of designing parks in the 1980's—albeit in very differing ways.

Chapter
Four

Parks and
Park Structures

PUBLIC SQUARE
WILKES-BARRE,
PENNSYLVANIA
Bohlin Powell
Brown Larkin Cywinski

The historic center of Wilkes-Barre is the Public Square, a big outdoor room set diagonally in the downtown street grid. The architects intensified its use as a green, oasis-like center by incorporating activities that range from resting and card playing to festivals and a weekly Farmers' Market.

Basic materials are similar throughout— red asphalt pavers, granite curbs and block pavers, painted steel—and they are used with great fun and verve, contrasting red and green granites, active patterns and "petroglyphs," and variations in scale. The original crossed pedestrian pattern has been retained, and its large trees have been supplemented by new

ones. The perimeter has been enlarged to allow for a ring of cherry trees set in raised granite planters, which buffer pedestrians from surrounding traffic and provide added seating. The "slots" between these planters harbor farmers' vehicles on market days. The square abounds in "focal points," but all are unified and tied together by a band of granite pavers that "twirls" around the block and into its center to circle a large illuminated fountain. Along its path, it links the planters accommodating the Farmers' Market, two striped granite restrooms, a performing area, and a small fountain set in a millstone-like granite disk.

The performing area is a recessed granite

Joseph Molitor photos

expanse, with stepped seating at its edge and a raised stage dramatized by a festive, variable backdrop: a three-dimensional, green-painted steel pipe truss, with changeable fabric panels secured to stainless steel disks.

From the larger scales of the canopy and the various activity centers, the architects have carried their design concerns down to the relatively minute scale of the steel "bent people seats" and the "petroglyphs" or "rock carvings" sprinkled along the granite paving blocks (see photos bottom right). Some 300 of these intaglio sculptures were specially designed and sandblasted into the walks; many of them have references to the flood, a map of the area, the history of the region, produce and animals from the Farmers' Market and the like (the one illustrated refers to coal mining in the region). However, the architects had a bit of "in" fun with a number of the carvings: plans of/by Mies, Ronchamp, Nowicki, Jefferson; sections of Kahn and Aalto; a Mackintosh flower, and various other "architecture" references. All-in-all, there are a lot of interests and "lures" to re-people the shops and streets.

SOUTH MAIN STREET/PUBLIC SQUARE URBAN DEVELOPMENTS. Owner: *City of Wilkes-Barre.* Client: *Redevelopment Authority of the City of Wilkes-Barre.* Architects and engineers: *Bohlin Powell Brown Larkin Cywinski—principals-in-charge: Peter Q. Bohlin, and Richard E. Powell;* project architect: *William Gladish;* project engineer: *Walter F. Blejwas, Jr.;* project team members: *David Wilson, Richard Shields, Edwin Gunshore, Eric Oliner.* Planners and urban designers: *Direction Associates.* Consultants: *Criterion Company* (structural engineering); *Paul H. Yeomans, Inc.* (electrical and plumbing engineering); *Huth Engineers, Inc.* (civil engineering); *John Brown* (landscape design); *David A. Mintz* (lighting); *Boles, Smyth Associates, Inc.* (traffic). General contractors: *American Asphalt Paving Company* (South Main Street); *Sordoni Construction Company* (Public Square).

Public Square, the center of Wilkes-Barre's downtown, has been re-designed to encourage a constant variety of activities: from oratory to drama and music in its amphitheater (photos top right and far left); strolling and relaxing along the tree-shaded walks and contemplating the fountains and "petroglyphs" (photos below right); playing games at the permanent tables and benches (top right in plan below); and a weekly outdoor Farmers' Market, when vehicles with meats and produce are installed between the raised planters surrounding the park (photos above and left).

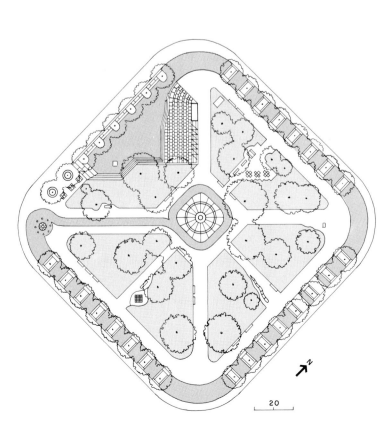

20

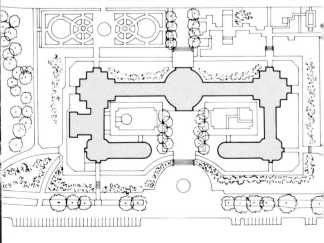

Top, the restored conservatory; left, the new bus drop off; right, north entrance; below, site plan. Overleaf, formal display house.

Alexandra Timchula photos

HAUPT CONSERVATORY NEW YORK BOTANICAL GARDEN BRONX, NEW YORK
Edward Larrabee Barnes

The Conservatory of the New York Botanical Garden must be the most otherworldly place in the Bronx—or anywhere else, for that matter. Set on a formal grassed podium, the turn of the century steel-and-glass structure rises off the lawn in white-boned translucent Beaux-Arts bubbles. At once tropical and Victorian, the low, arched, domed building, full of exotic flora, seems to belong in some Jamesian era of crinolines and bizarre feathered hats. Begun in 1899 and attributed to William R. Cobb, architect for the still-extant greenhouse manufacturers Lord and Burnham, the recently-landmarked Conservatory is a rare and lovely example of a period greenhouse C-shaped in plan. The atmospheric beauty of this cathedral built to nature inspires not only fantasy but awe; the building commands respectful attention, both for itself and for the man-made Eden it shelters from the real Bronx outside.

It's hard to believe, but true, that a little over five years ago the structure was considered a white elephant by the Garden, and was threatened with demolition. After all, administrators argued, the building had been remodeled twice in 1938 and 1953, with results judged disastrous with accelerating rapidity. The '30s restoration, reflecting the drastic change in taste since the beginning of the century, stripped the building of its ornate cresting and simplified its Victorian detail; fifteen years later, the Park Service severely mutilated the building, hacking off two Italian Renaissance vestibules to replace them with a brick wall and WPA-style entry.

So, in the heyday of what New York cultural institutions remember as the Hoving era, and City Hall recalls as the Lindsay epoch—a time of grand plans for cultural facilities—the Garden called in the architectural firm of Edward Larrabee Barnes to do a new master plan with a view to eliminating the Conservatory and constructing a new building on the site. To Barnes's credit, he supported the minority preservationist call to save and renovate the Conservatory. But subsequent changes in policy and funding have meant that while the Conservatory has been restored, the rest of Barnes's plan, including his project for the new Plants and Man building, is on indefinite hold.

Begun in piecemeal fashion on a shoestring city budget, the Conservatory's restoration was completed thanks to a gift from Enid Annenberg Haupt. This funding supported a thorough structural and mechanical rehauling, but did not allow for any "luxuries," esthetic or technical.

The most devastating consequence of the cutback in the master plan was that the restored Conservatory would have to house the educational exhibits originally intended for the Plants and Man building and handle the traffic that these entail. Barnes, who looked forward to restoring the Conservatory to its former leisurely elegance, complete with decorative gar-

dens, is undisguisedly "regretful that this building had to become a large-scale teaching facility."

One particularly disturbing result of the expanded function of the Conservatory is a radical alteration of the circulation scheme. Originally, one approached the conservatory in processional Beaux-Arts style, passing between the enclosing wings, through the courtyard and into the domed central pavilion. From here one strolled through either ell, reversed direction and returned to repeat the promenade on the other side. This radial circulation pattern, however conducive to contemplation of the flora, simply won't work, the Garden realized at the last minute, for large groups. Accordingly, the Garden requested the architects to link the two end greenhouses by a tunnel, creating an efficient circulation loop (see plan page 64) but "severely damaging the architectural experience of the building"—as Barnes has pointed out.

This tunnel, done at rock-bottom cost, is a galvanized steel culvert-type connection curved in an onion shape: Necessary as it is, this crude element forms a jarring contrast with the elegant domes of steel tracery above. So, unfortunately, does a second structural intervention necessitated by the educational program: a large cement stair leading to a basement teaching area below house 1 (plan, overleaf).

The damage to the Beaux-Arts axiality and the sequential ordering of the spaces is compounded by the present entrance, into a corner pavilion. Barnes has, however, done a good deal to correct this problem, and to recapture the axes, in reorienting the approaches to the building. One now enters the Garden and approaches the conservatory via a new main entrance (photo, preceding spread). Designed as a bus and auto drop off, the eye shaped entrance is outlined by a curved wall, an eyebrow of Cyclopean masonry that seems to rise out of the natural rock outcroppings at the right, becoming progressively manmade in appearance. The wall, and the planted berm behind it, are pierced by a pedestrian tunnel; moving through this passage, those approaching on foot lose the roar of the street and emerge in the green garden.

Barnes has also endeavored to re-establish an axial entrance to the Conservatory itself (plan, overleaf). When ongoing road work is completed, visitors will approach the building from what was originally the rear, entering on axis on the north side of the central pavilion.

The north side, one of the highlights of the exterior renovation, is quite worthy to welcome visitors (photo, bottom right, preceding spread). Both the original entrance vestibules to the central greenhouse were essentially demolished in the brutal '58 remodeling; and the original working drawings had been lost. From old photographs and a few original, not very detailed drawings, project architect Siglinde Stern reconstructed the vestibules inside and out. Because of budgetary constraints, the original cast-iron facades of the vestibules had to be rebuilt in cast aluminum, and the decorative paning, both here and in the fan windows, was replaced by sheet glass with metal filigree work superimposed. Although some corners were cut in the final realization (some of the planned filigree was omitted, leaving the larger panes a bit bleak) the effect is nonetheless one of magnificence.

Though the restoration of the vestibules may be the most visible and, from a historical point of view, the most impressive part of the project, the fundamental, meat-and-potatoes work was concerned with the structural and mechanical systems. In a slowly-moving sequential renovation, each piece of the steel was stripped, tested, and, if necessary, replaced. The glass skin underwent a similar process. The existing mullions had replaced the original Victorian mullions in 1938, when the elaborate six-mullioned bays were altered to a simpler module of four mullions. The extant mullions, however, constituted a sophisticated response to the problems posed by the humid interior. Each of the galvanized metal U-sections had cypress inserts, into which the glass was set with putty. (Cypress is one of two woods naturally resistant to damp—the other being the much softer redwood.) Each

A Partition, historical display house

B New stairs to lower level

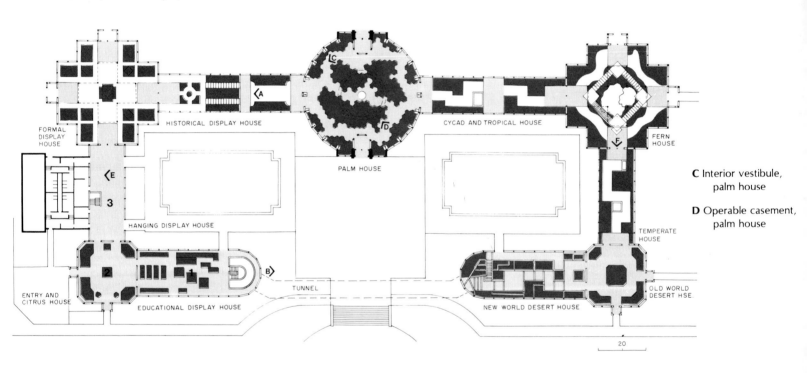

FORMAL DISPLAY HOUSE

HISTORICAL DISPLAY HOUSE

PALM HOUSE

HANGING DISPLAY HOUSE

ENTRY AND CITRUS HOUSE

EDUCATIONAL DISPLAY HOUSE

TUNNEL

CYCAD AND TROPICAL HOUSE

FERN HOUSE

TEMPERATE HOUSE

NEW WORLD DESERT HOUSE

OLD WORLD DESERT HSE.

20

C Interior vestibule, palm house

D Operable casement, palm house

F Catwalk, fern house

E Mirror wall, hanging display house

cypress-lined mullion was carefully repaired and re-used: where this was not possible, redwood was substituted. The alternative—to replace the steel-and-wood mullions with modern aluminum ones—"would have made the whole building fat," as Barnes puts it; the thicker bands of soft metal would have destroyed the fine strong lines of the steel frame.

Concentrating on essentials, the architects also modernized heating, wiring, and piping systems. In addition to replacing and repairing roof and side wall ventilators, the architects made several of the large vertical windows operable, creating badly-needed ventilation. In an intervention as simply beautiful as it is ingenious, the architects devised a manually operable wheel- and-gear system to open the huge casements. Reminiscent of early industrial window opening systems and of such famous early modern offspring of these as Le Corbusier's window systems in the Maison de Verre, the hand-operable, visible mechanism is a sophisticated recapturing, on a small scale, of the somewhat naive delight in the machine, and in man's ability to tune the built environment, which the Conservatory itself embodies.

Lastly, a small and relatively spontaneous structural alteration combines efficiency with esthetics. A new boiler house, done just before Barnes came to the job, met the Conservatory with a brick-walled intrusion, enclosing a stair, and sealed off that side of greenhouse 3 (see plan) with a blank wall. Cutting down the stairwell so that its brick edge appears to be another planter, project architect Alistair Bevington also conceived of duplicating, on the partition separating the greenhouse from the offices (also housed within the walls of the boiler structure) the elevation of the glass wall opposite, which gives on to the court. The "fake," realized in mirrored one-way glass, so that those in the offices can see without being seen, visually opens up that side of the greenhouse (photo, bottom center, opposite).

Moreover, constructing an "outside" wall on an interior partition is perfectly in the spirit of the original architecture. The varied prisms of the eleven greenhouses that compose the conservatory meet each other with no intermediary concessions; the skin of the domed polygonal volumes continues uninterrupted across the space enclosed by the long vaulted elements. The outside wall, unchanged, becomes interior divider in the middle of a fan window (photo, top left, opposite). This simple additive method of construction, in which one greenhouse is just stuck on to the next, creates serendipitously sophisticated architecture by throwing into high relief the ambiguities of this glass house, inside which man makes the outside of his dreams, a nature tamed, ordered, and made to do tricks. In a greenhouse, inside *is* outside.

Details like the reconstruction of the vestibules, the window systems and the mirror wall exemplify the sensitive spirit of this restoration. The renovation of this spectacular yet terribly delicate landmark called for no grand costly gestures, no daring juxtapositions of new and old, no flamboyant innovation, but rather for a quiet, direct rebuilding of the original. Barnes's office has carried out repairs and renovations with a necessary economy of means which seems to have sparked a small wealth of invention. The restoration preserves the elusive, unquantifiable exhilaration of the architecture, and the shimmering domes retain a younger century's poignant marveling at man's capacity to fashion a machine-house for making a garden in.

ENID A. HAUPT CONSERVATORY, New York Botanical Garden, Bronx, New York. Architects: *Edward Larrabee Barnes—associates-in-charge: Percy Keck, Alistair Bevington; project architects: Siglinde Stern, Michael Timchula, Hillary Brown.* Consultants: *Weidlinger Associates* (structural soils); *Arthur Edwards* (mechanical electrical); *David Klepper* (acoustical); *Donald Bliss* (lighting); *Vignelli Associates* (graphics). Landscape architects: *Kiley, Tindall, Walker—partner in-charge: Peter Walker.* General contractor: *Louisa Construction Co., Inc.—superintendent: Angelo Sisca.*

FRANKLIN-WRIGHT SETTLEMENTS CAMP ORION TOWNSHIP, MICHIGAN
Rossen/Neumann Associates

After six decades of rough-and-tumble summertime wear had taken their toll on the Franklin-Wright Settlements Camp, a nonprofit facility in Michigan for underprivileged children, the camp administrators decided that periodic "Band-Aid" repairs were no longer adequate. They turned to Rossen/Neumann Associates for master planning of low-cost renovations and new buildings on the 82-acre lakeside site. The architects advised that the first priority for economic survival should be a reorientation of the camp towards rental use by other groups from autumn to spring. Construction began with housing, the camp's most pressing need. Each of the first three cottages built comprises six bunk rooms grouped in pairs, with dividing doors for flexibility and interconnecting lavatories adaptable for use by one or both sexes. Windows at child-height and adult eyelevel let campers of any age enjoy the view (upper right). Adjoining common rooms are a place to meet on rainy days or between scheduled activities. Owing to stringent state fire codes, the architects had to specify a

higher degree of interior finish than they originally desired. Since rustic paneling was unfeasible, lively supergraphics were painted on tough plywood walls. Outside, the frame structures were clad with cedar shakes, stained gray and bleached to an appropriately weathered shade. In order to reinforce a sense of community, the cabins face into a central gathering place, an open hearth surrounded by raised platforms, with plenty of room for marshmallow roasts, skits, and singalongs. Counselors have nicknamed this structure "the pagoda" because its four gateways remind them of oriental temple portals. The analogy is curiously apt, befitting a place reserved for rituals of fellowship.

FRANKLIN-WRIGHT SETTLEMENTS CAMP, Orion Township, Michigan. Owner: *Franklin-Wright Settlements, Inc.* Architects: *Rossen/Neumann Associates—David F. Dombroski, AIA, project designer; J. Victor Muñoz, AIA, project manager.* Engineers: *Sheppard Engineering* (structural), *Fuerstenberg, Crompton & Associates, Inc.* (mechanical/electrical). General contractor: *Roberts & Dudlar, Inc.*

The three cottages completed in the first phase of construction house 90 campers. Interconnecting rooms can be combined into suites to accommodate the needs of families and organizations who rent the camp before and after the summer session. A common room and sheltered terrace in each cottage furnish intermediate social areas between the relative privacy of bunkhouses and the central "public" platform where camp assemblies are held (left and below right). The master plan conceived by Rossen/Neumann Associates recommends later construction of a second cluster of cabins, permitting the separation of boys' and girls' campsites. When funding is available, a 15-year-old lodge will be remodeled as a dining hall and focus for an outdoor commons and recreation ground.

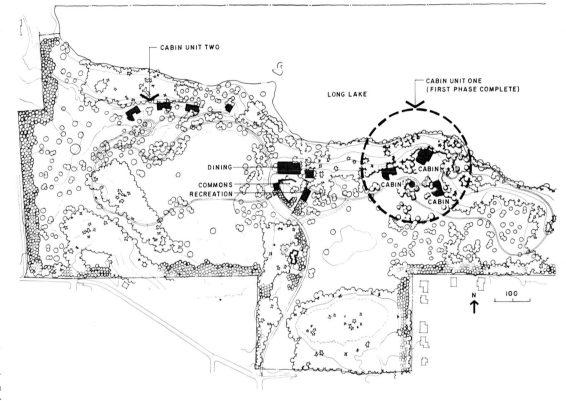

CABIN UNIT TWO

CABIN UNIT ONE (FIRST PHASE COMPLETE)

LONG LAKE

DINING

COMMONS RECREATION

CABIN

N 100

©Timothy Hursley/B. Korab, Ltd. photos

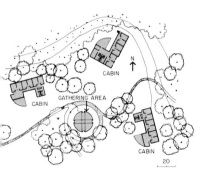

CABIN

CABIN

GATHERING AREA

N

CABIN

20

VISITORS' CENTER
CHICAGO HORTICULTURAL SOCIETY
GLENCOE, ILLINOIS
Edward Larrabee Barnes

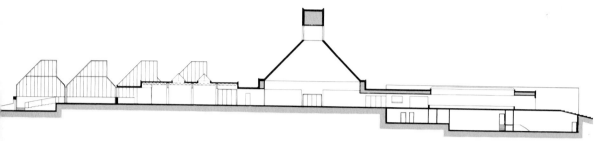

©Nick Wheeler photos

The site chosen for the new Botanic Garden for the Chicago Horticultural Society was a 320-acre low land area consisting mainly of unused swampy meadow land, depleted farms and extraction pits at the head of the Skokie Lagoon complex in Glencoe, Illinois about 50 miles north of Chicago. The land was acquired from the Cook Country Forest Preserve District. The master plan, which established the major land use and circulation patterns for the entire site, was prepared by Environmental Planning and Design, the landscape architecture and planning firm founded by John Ormsbee and Philip Douglas Simonds. The Simonds brothers and their partners and associates developed the site over a 14-year period beginning in 1963. They converted it into a new and beautiful setting of garden islands surrounded by lagoons and meandering waterways. Edward Larrabee Barnes was commissioned in 1970 to design the Administration and Visitors Center to occupy the largest of these islands.

If Barnes had designed his building in the spirit of this landscape he probably would have devised a rather random and yielding asymmetrical pattern. Instead he chose to develop a formal, axial, symmetrical solution, deliberately classic, in juxtaposition to the romantic forms of the landscape. Defined as a separate and distinct precinct by the strict geometry of the 30-foot-wide berm that forms its boundaries, the building appears from the air like a multi-faceted jewel on a patch of moss surrounded by still water.

Although a building of such crystalline order might better command the vistas of an Italian Renaissance garden than dominate a mounded and curving

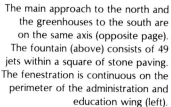

The main approach to the north and the greenhouses to the south are on the same axis (opposite page). The fountain (above) consists of 49 jets within a square of stone paving. The fenestration is continuous on the perimeter of the administration and education wing (left).

landscape ever so suggestive of Japanese temple gardens, there is a certain *frisson* in the manner in which it contradicts its surroundings. To disagree is always harder than to concur and by electing to juxtapose rather than to harmonize, Barnes set himself a difficult task. His building has its own deliberate contradictions, its rooms focus inward, yet its axes open upon extended outward vistas. From the exterior the building appears sealed and contained, like a ship, but from within it invites the surrounding land and lakes.

Barnes imposed this order upon a very complex program. The Administration and Visitors Center serves adults and children, groups and individuals, amateurs and professionals. It is the administrative center for the entire garden. Seminar rooms, classrooms, a small auditorium for 200, a library, an exhibition hall, a cluster of greenhouses, outdoor exhibition spaces, offices, simple dining facilities, delivery and staging space have been arranged so that they can be operated independently or as a unit. This flexible and versatile building has been organized into a cruciform plan approached on

foot from the east and by car from the west.

The exhibition hall with its pyramid shaped tent-like roof and its high monitor skylight marks the center, and the cloistered courtyards on each side to the east and west separate the complex into two areas: to the south greenhouses and service and to the north administration and education. The west courtyard contains a fountain, which consists of 49 jets rising directly from a square of stone paving. On special occasions the large exhibition hall can be thrown open to these two courtyards

In this building as in almost all of his work, Barnes has strictly limited his range of materials and colors as can be seen in the photos on this and the opposite page. He has used buff limestone for copings, greenhouse sills and landscape details and in combination with iron spot brick for interior and exterior paving. The walls are of Chicago common sewer brick and the ceilings are of western hemlock in narrow slats. These slatted ceilings are used in the cloisters (right), the main exhibition hall, and the exhibition areas around the greenhouses. The wood was given a fire retardant coating. The greenhouse pavilions are modified pyramids, echoing the shape of the main exhibition hall roof.

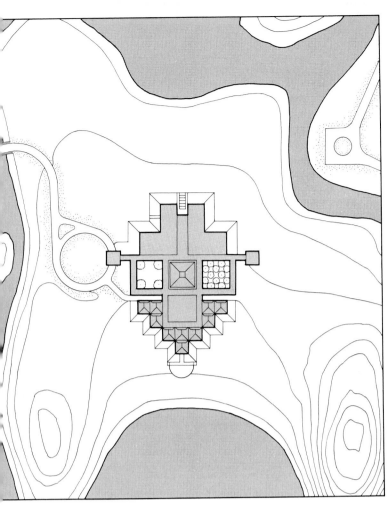

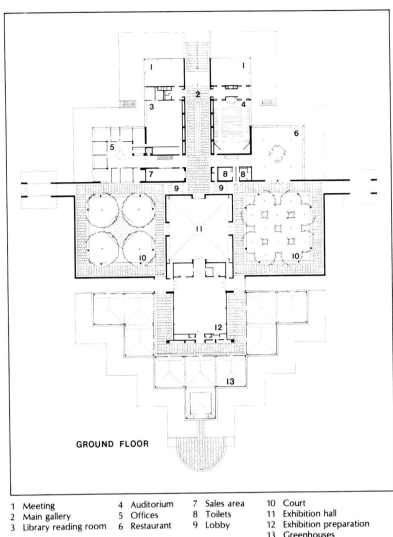

GROUND FLOOR

1 Meeting	4 Auditorium	7 Sales area	10 Court
2 Main gallery	5 Offices	8 Toilets	11 Exhibition hall
3 Library reading room	6 Restaurant	9 Lobby	12 Exhibition preparation
			13 Greenhouses

creating a continuous indoor-outdoor space extending 280 feet along the east-west axis.

To the north of the exhibition hall on the north-south axis is a long brick gallery with a central reflecting pool, a skylight above and glass doors opening out to a lake. This gallery isolates the library and administrative offices from the noise of the cafe and lecture hall.

The entire building is one story except for a small basement to the north of the exhibition hall and courtyards. All mechanical equipment is located there including the air-conditioning system which uses water from the lagoon. The entire building is air conditioned except for the greenhouses. These greenhouses are clustered in three adjoining groups around a work area beyond the exhibition pavilion on the southern end of the main axis. They are linked by a cloister-like exhibition space between work area and the greenhouse entrances. The southernmost house has a wide stair leading to a lower level and out at the southern extremity of the complex onto a semi-circular brick paved terrace.

A simple palette of four harmonizing materials has been used throughout the public spaces. All the walls are of a soft pink to buff Chicago select common brick. The paving consists of large areas of buff-colored dolomitic limestone from Minnesota bordered and floating in straw-colored iron spot brick pavers. The ceilings of the exhibition hall and cloisters are of natural wood slatted panels. The only other significant visible materials are mullionless glass used in all the windows and entrance doors and natural copper for the roofs of the exhibition hall and entrance canopy.

ADMINISTRATION AND VISITORS CENTER, Botanic Garden of the Chicago Horticultural Society, Glencoe, Illinois. Architect: *Edward Larrabee Barnes—associate-in-charge: Alistair Bevington; project architect: Gajinder Singh.* Consultants: *Severud, Perrone, Sturm, Conlin, Bandel* (structural); *Cosentini Associates* (mechanical/electrical); *Klepper, Marshal, King* (acoustical); *Donald Bliss* (lighting); *Mary Barnes of Edward Larrabee Barnes Office* (interiors); *Wolf & Company, Hanscomb Roy* (costs); *Ickes-Braun* (greenhouse). General contractor: *Coath & Goss—superintendent of construction: Fred Bock.*

In the main exhibition hall (above), the slatted surfaces
on the walls and ceiling have acoustic backing.
The building can be said to have only two continuous windows,
each nearly 250 feet long and four feet high. These
windows (opposite page, top left) are butt glazed
with no vertical mullions for the entire length.
There are central skylights in the restaurant (top right),
the entrance concourse (left) and the office area.

103

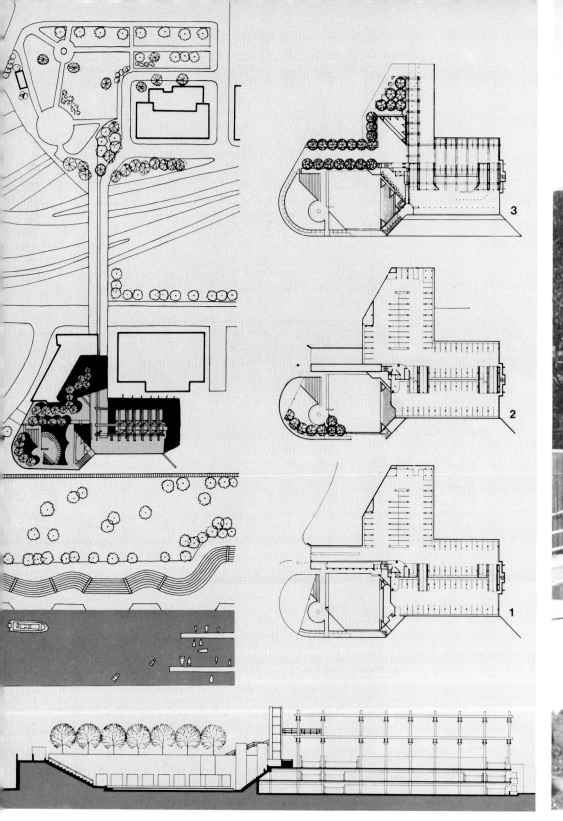

CINCINNATUS FORUM
CINCINNATI, OHIO
Louis Sauer Associates

Robert Lautman photos, except as noted

Cut off by a major arterial from the central business district, sections of Cincinnati's riverfront had gradually slipped into the familiar pattern of less and less use until city officials, determined to redeem these potentially valuable properties, embarked on an ambitious program of reclamation. In order to encourage public use of one such area, they commissioned Louis Sauer Associates to design a rather complex amenity: a recreational concourse and plaza, shown in the site plan above, that are intended to string together a large riverfront complex: shops, restaurants, and a residential tower on the site's northwest corner.

The new park is tied back to the central business district at several points but most importantly by a combined pedestrian and vehicular bridge that spans the expressway. Pedestrians arrive at a broad elevated plaza that overlooks the river while automobiles are collected in a 200-car parking garage under the plaza. From the plaza, pedestrians descend into an enchanting urban garden of trees and shrubs, of sculptured concrete masses, of terraces and stepping stones, of waterworks developed in a variety of ways. These are "people spaces" of a sophisticated character; spaces that almost demand the viewer's active participation; spaces that are

designed to seem incomplete, like an empty stage set, without that participation.

Water, of course, is a remarkably adaptable design medium and Sauer has used it in a range of expressions from static and serene to active—even aggressive. At the lively end of this spectrum is a huge water cannon (photo above) that fires volleys of spray in changing patterns through an adjustable cluster of nozzles.

Water is also a powerful recruiter. In warm weather, citizens—some who might otherwise be opening hydrants—stream to the site, shedding their shoes to wade, to refresh their faces, and a few to test the force

of the water cannon itself. The stepped cascade, which carries water from the four concrete towers down to the lower level pool, is designed quite specifically for use by bathers (photo upper right). On more than one occasion, the park has been so popular that health officials have been forced to close it down temporarily to thin out huge crowds.

Around and through this watery landscape are ramps, grassy berms and built-in street furniture to which participants can retreat when the urge overtakes them.

At the east end of the site, a large and powerful concrete trellis signals arrival and

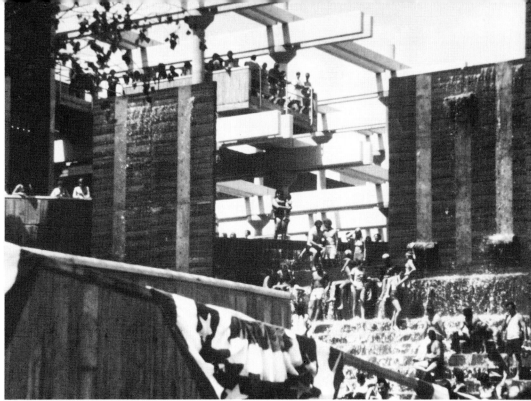

Louis Sauer

Louis Sauer

echoes faintly in its form the structural vocabulary of nearby bridges that span the Ohio River. It is here in this processional space that rows of shops and restaurants add another dimension to the project and serve the adjacent residential community. The trellis structure can expand eastward in modular increments as new demands may arise.

In mid-fall, when the waterworks are shut down, the character of the park changes, of course, but it remains until the onset of really cold weather an active playground and significant urban magnet. Completed in 1978, at a cost of about $3 million, the park continues to be enormously popular with a wide range of ages and income groups and makes an important contribution to the life of the city. It is a design that dares a great deal, and a design with many lessons for architects, for sociologists, for all those—whether professional or not—whose interest is the urban habitat.

CINCINNATUS FORUM, Cincinnati, Ohio. Architect: *Louis Sauer Associates—David Brossart, project architect.* Engineers: *Bernard Schwartz & Associates* (structural), *Maxfield, Edwards & Backer* (mechanical/electrical). Urban sociologist: *John Zeisel.* Consultant: *Ralph H. Burke* (parking). Contractor: *Frank Messer & Sons.*

As places for people's enjoyment, marketplaces are a relatively new concept, although their roots are deep in history. As assemblies of diverse small entrepreneurs competing to capture the customer's eye, marketplaces motivated the founding of the first villages and towns. In rural societies, they provided the pleasurable side benefit of seeing other people, along with the performances of traveling troubadours and minstrels, while filling their basic function: necessary distribution of commodities.

After decades of neglect, the marketplace concept has been revived, and designers use the once-secondary appeal of an animated gathering place as a primary attraction to get business for shops and restaurants. Located in or among new or colorfully renovated older buildings, the successful marketplace produces a festive air by careful design, the nature of the participating businesses and often by some programmed entertainments that range from performing clowns to concerts.

As distinct from shopping malls, marketplaces are often designed around a focal space, and the businesses are open to or part of it. However, this plan is not the only one, and design can encourage the concept in a number of different configurations.

There are three basic forms that marketplaces can take — sheds, arcades and streets. Washington's Market House (the first project on the following pages) is a classic example of the shed. But the really ambitious 19th-century city looked to the dramatic galleries and arcades of contemporary Europe for inspiration. The Cleveland Arcade in Cleveland, Ohio (see jacket) is the largest such arcade in the United States. Architects Kaplan/McLaughlin/Diaz are in the process of restoring it to its former grandeur. Herbert McLaughlin has a dual role as architect and partner in the development firm of Conner, McLaughlin & Oppmann. He says that the Arcade is really more of an ancestor of the shopping mall than a market, because its commercial activities were discreetly concealed behind storefronts that ringed the multi-story central space. Still, the drama of this space — and the social activities that occur in it—give the building a focus that must have been even more pronounced when it was "the only show in town."

The nature of the shops and restaurants helps create the festive atmosphere. While the basic purpose of the new marketplace remains, like the old, commerce, it is commerce of a very different sort. The merchandise is no longer basic necessities, but special items meant to delight the eye of the buyer at leisure. Good restaurants and bars put the buyer in the proper mood, and contribute to the feeling that this is in fact a special place.

Several projects in this chapter show the kinds of marketplaces that can be created in new buildings. One is Harborplace in Baltimore, by Benjamin Thompson & Associates (who may be said to have started the revival of the marketplace concept with their development of Boston's Faneuil Hall in the mid-seventies). Harborplace demonstrates how marketplace buildings can fulfill urban planning roles. Another is Citicorp Center, which demonstrates how other types of buildings (this one is a major office building) can contribute to urban liveliness by embracing the marketplace concept on their lower floors. But the remodeling of older structures seems to be the most usual way that new marketplaces are created — perhaps because the older structures offer the easiest route to the necessary ingredient of unique character.

Chapter Five

Urban Marketplaces

MARKET HOUSE
WASHINGTON, DC
Clark Tribble Harris & Li

Built as a market in 1865 for what was then the separate suburb of Georgetown, this small building is a classic survivor of the covered centralized marketplace boasted by most small towns in the United States at that time. Despite its relatively modest size—40 by 200 feet—it was long the local hub of commercial and social activity. Because farmers stopped coming there to set up their stalls around 1935, its existence was threatened. It was protected, however, by covenants on site usage in the original deed, and it stumbled further into the twentieth century as the Square Deal Supermarket and then as a wholesale auto-parts distributorship.

In their plan to revitalize Markethouse on more traditional lines, architects Clark Tribble Harris & Li have employed current retailing techniques that once more make a social setting work. According to partner Jerry Li: "You have to give the clientele what it can't get in supermarkets—whether it's a special ambiance or unusual merchandise." The architects have opted for a lot of both. And it is interesting to compare the ways they have done this here to similar patterns at the much larger Harborplace to be dicussed later on. As discussed in the caption, there are careful controls of lighting and tenant graphics and a tight circulation system that is uniquely desirable in this type of retailing. Awnings both inside and outside of windows help to control natural light in order to heighten the theatrical effect and to present a consistent design.

At the official opening recently, nineteen diverse food operations occupied spaces ranging in size from 72 to 530 square feet. These included butchers and green-grocers, purveyors of condiments and ready-made hors d'oeuvres to full meals, and a restaurant on the mezzanine to overlook the whole busy scene. The colorful result has a rich vibrant character and a liveliness that make it a place where people want to be.

THE MARKET HOUSE, Washington, D.C. Owner: *joint venture of the Western Development Corporation and the Donohoe Companies.* Architects: *Clark Tribble Harris & Li.* Engineers: *Tadjer-Cohen* (structural); *Gormley-Wareham Associates* (mechanical/electrical) *Vinsant Associates* (tenant mechancial/electrical). Consultants: *Peter Barna/Lighting Design* (lighting); *Design/Joe Sonderman Inc.* (graphics). General contractor: *Western Construction Company.*

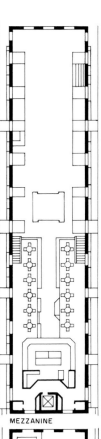

MEZZANINE

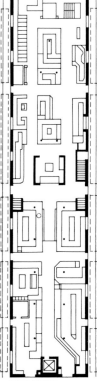

MAIN FLOOR

Despite the seeming casualness here, there is a design formula that similar plans would do well to heed. Architect Li likens the result to a stage set. Instead of supermarket-sized corridors, there are narrow ones that invite people to see the merchandise and each other at close range. Instead of bright even lighting, there are directed pinpoints that highlight the special nature of what is being sold. Instead of rows of standardized displays, there is a variety of stands with individual graphics, both encouraged and controlled by the architects to add to the bazaar-like flavor.

WASHINGTON BOULEVARD IMPROVEMENT AREA DETROIT, MICHIGAN
Rossetti Associates

©Timothy Hursley/B. Korab, Ltd.

One of two similar projects by architects Rossetti Associates for contiguous streets meeting at Cadillac Square, this dramatic transformation was done to re-establish two qualities that were seen as vital to the once-fashionable thoroughfare's revival. One quality involved imagery; it was elegance. Until the early 1960s, this had been spelled out by islands of flowers and bronze statues down the center of an eight-lane Baron-Haussmann style boulevard, once bordered by stylish shops and cafes on wide sidewalks occupied by a bustling clientele and leisurely strollers. Such places fulfill an elite variation on the urban marketplace as defined in the introduction to this Study. And especially for large cities, such a variation is no less important to the lifeblood of excitement.

But because times had greatly changed for Washington Boulevard, more was needed than to re-establish imagery. Accordingly, the second thrust of the architects' work involved planning that would bring back a street life. The basic planning decision was to put the pervasive automobile at arm's length for some space to breathe and move. Accordingly, the width of the street was shrunk to four lanes of two-way traffic on the western side of the original central islands. And the land thus retrieved was combined with that occupied by the islands to form a five-block-long urban park, full of varied pedestrian spaces, and projected cafes.

According to project designer Jim Andal; "Rossetti's work here will not be judged in terms of design, but in terms of the influence it has in turning around the decline of a once-great avenue." And things *are* happening. While there are still lots of empty retail and commercial space, a new residential project is beginning construction, and hotel occupancy has stabilized, both bringing the promise of a renewed liveliness to the boulevard.

WASHINGTON BOULEVARD IMPROVEMENT AREA, Detroit, Michigan. Owner: *City of Detroit.* Architects: *Rossetti Associates/Architects Planners—Gino Rossetti, Jim Amdal (designers); John Malak (production/project management); Al Fraser (project management).* Engineers: *McClurg and Associates, Inc.* (structural); *DiClemente-Siegel Engineers* (electrical/mechanical); *Urban Engineering Company* (civil). Landscape architects: *James C. Scott and Associates.* General contractor: *Waterford Construction.*

The imagery that architect Rossetti has brought to Washington Boulevard is both elegant and definitely of the twentieth century. Over 3,000 feet of red-painted steel trellis-like structures contribute to the style of the project and help to define the various spaces. They also carry a strip of distinctive lighting. The central block (seen in the aerial view) employs water in varied pools and fountains that extend up into the trellises. At the Grand River intersection (background of aerial and photo right) a circular light-sculpture by Jim Pallas responds to motion and sound. One location for the projected outdoor cafes, that will complete the desired liveliness, is under this sculpture. An old-fashioned trolley threads through the whole, and encourages decreased dependence on automobiles. The result is meant to be a high-quality framework for a linear version of the urban marketplace.

HARBORPLACE
BALTIMORE, MARYLAND
Benjamin Thompson & Associates

Clemens Kalischer

Baltimore has poured a lot of energy and money into building a new center for its business district near the harbor. Starting in 1958, some $180 million of private and public pre-inflationary monies were spent on the 33-acre Charles Center alone. Current plans for the downtown area project an ultimate investment of $1.25 billion. But until now, the missing ingredient has been a sense of marketplace liveliness that would provide a focus, and unify downtown.

Harborplace is such a focus. Thanks to architects Benjamin Thompson & Associates and the developer, the Rouse Company, two new waterside pavilions are already functioning as a traditional marketplace—an active town center, although problems of access across the busy surrounding streets have yet to be resolved. Almost 250,000 square feet of restaurants, cafes, retail stores, stands and kiosks are producing at last a vivid street life. And the fact that they can do this is a major part of the story of their design. It is a story that proves that—in the right hands—completely new construction can fulfill historic roles, without necessarily bringing along the historic trappings.

In form and scale, the two new buildings of the complex have a strong resemblance to the wharf buildings that once occupied the site (bottom photo). Even the pennants that fly from the new roofs are replicas of those once used to signal which ships were berthed at the moment. According to Jane Thompson, "We remembered the tradition of commercial waterfront construction: shed-like warehouses and covered piers, ferry terminals, yacht clubs and waterfront grandstands for viewing races and regattas. We also remembered the great tradition of America's major city parks, once animated by dramatic greenhouses, horticultural halls and exposition buildings. There is no attempt at an architectural 'style' here. If anything, it is post-post modern. There are no tacked-on decorations. Everything you see comes from basic considerations of how the project would work best for its modern purpose."

For instance, the "porticos" that interrupt the linearity of the shed-like roofs make places for people to see through the buildings, and encourage them to come in from both sides. The transparency of the exterior walls allows views of interior activity, and—at the porticos—helps to carry through one of

The concrete and steel-roof framed pavilions are a major part of an ambitious people-oriented waterfront development planned by Wallace Roberts & Todd. This includes a park that is to stretch from the western building (left in aerial view and sketch perspective) around two sides of the harbor. It is to be lushly planted with trees. And according to Benjamin Thompson: Both the trees to be planted in front of the new buildings and the color of the new standing-seam aluminum roofs are meant to carry the future belt of green along the shore on this side of the harbor. The historic frigate *S.S. Constellation* is permanently moored, and the wide plaza between the two new buildings is meant to open diagonal vistas to the habor and the frigate from the center of town.

©Steve Rosenthal photos except as noted

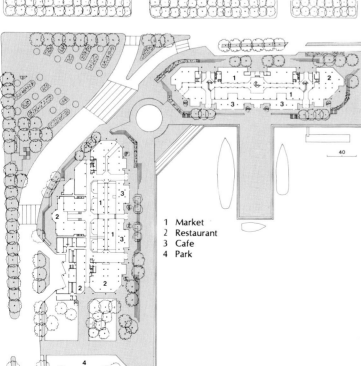

1 Market
2 Restaurant
3 Cafe
4 Park

40

115

Clemens Kalischer

the basic design considerations: "to embrace the shore without blocking it." The promenades that connect these porticos at the second-floor levels reinforce the nineteenth-century proportions, and fulfill both the historic and modern functions of giving people places to view the passing scene, while they stroll or relax in outdoor cafes. The sloping roofs of the exterior "greenhouses" came from the need for temporary structures over utility easements in some locations. The high sloping roofs of the main buildings conceal mechanical equipment.

Roughly the size of Thompson and Rouse's prototypical (and enormously successful Faneuil Hall Marketplace in Boston, Harborplace has already achieved a comparable volume of business. It was an instant commercial as well as social success. All of this is due to some very careful and by now expert decisions by both architects and developers. A variety of businesses was encouraged, and those most different from each other were often placed side by side. The architects call it "a mixed-use marketplace." There is a distinct difference, however, in the commercial thrust of each of the two buildings that constitute the market.

Clemens Kalischer

The northern pavilion has a narrow central corridor that widens where it meets the vertical circulation inside the porticos. The purpose is both social and commercial: to bring people close to each other and the merchandise. This pavilion houses established specialty shops and some of the more formal restaurants and cafes.

Clemens Kalischer

More open in plan, the western pavilion mostly houses food: quick service stands and kiosks, produce, fish and meat markets, more restaurants and various food specialty shops. In order to ensure the sale of less profitable produce, fish and meats, a raised low-rent aisle especially for their display runs down the center, and ties in with fast-food operations on the sides. One section of this pavilion is devoted to craft sales, and can be rented on a trial basis with one-month leases. Here, the architects have supplied complete facilities, while the spontaneous natures of some of the businesses, such as a kite store, have supplied some of the more novel graphics.

With such a mix in the western building there was a chance that both the quality of the stores and their graphics might not be up

According to Ben Thompson, It was very important that the new buildings have equal faces with no fronts or backs. This was a major reason for their pavilion-like qualities, that work so well for both their planning and functional roles. Still, the concept was not easy to sell to even such astute clients as Rouse. The traditional shopping center has a back for garbage and deliveries, and a front with limited entrances, so that people will pass by all of the shops to reach the anchors at the ends. Of course, this would have worked against the site's basic assets and tended to block the harbor from downtown, instead of opening it up.

to standard. But the commercial and visual planning success at Harborplace results from careful control of what businesses may lease and how they should look when they get there. According to Thompson's associate-in-charge Bruno D'Agostino: "The rush to get occupants in may have helped us even on the long-term shops. All of the storefronts, basic stands and storage facilities were provided by the developer as we designed them. Unlike the practice in shopping centers, there was a basic framework for individual additions and modifications. These facilities were sold to the tenants as they moved in.

Where did all the seemingly pent-up demand at Harborplace came from? According to Sandra Hillman, director of the Baltimore Promotion and Tourism office, fully 50 per cent of the people who came to the adjacent World Trade Center observatory are from out of town. Clearly, such attractions grouped together become a tourist magnet—and will become more of one now that the National Aquarium is complete on a nearby site.

Considering its vast popular success, it is surprising that there was so much opposition to the project before it was built. According to Ben Thompson; "We exhibited a model for three months before a referendum occurred in an anti-construction atmosphere. A lot of people thought there shouldn't have been any construction on the site at all—that it should be left open for the people." But it is clearly not just the architects and the developer who won the referendum; it was people as well. Overnight, Harborplace has become the major cultural and recreational activity in a downtown that desperately needed one.

By careful design control with a broad approach, the architects have created interior spaces that are neither rigid nor disordered. The results are what was wanted—a fresh and festive air. And from noon to late at night, when the buildings are often mobbed, the bright but controlled graphics clarify the rich visual impressions. A view of a cross aisle in the western building (right) and other views in the same building (top and bottom) reveal the high level of visual control, despite the input of many individual entrepreneurs, often in open stalls. A more closed plan with narrow aisles in the northern building (left and below) is meant to bring people in closer proximity to the merchandise and each other.

HARBORPLACE, Baltimore, Maryland. The Rouse Company. Architects: *Benjamin Thompson & Associates, Inc.*—partner-in-charge: *Bruno D'Agostino;* project architect: *Charles Izzo;* interior architect: *Wendy Tinker;* project team: *E. Diehl, J. Thompson, J. Piatt, K. Shapiro, T. Quirk, J. Van Sickle, D. Chilinski, R. Bernstein, B. Millham, I. Bereznicki.* Engineers: *Gilum-Colaco* (structural); *Robert G. Balter Co.* (soils); *Poole and Kent* (plumbing); *Joseph R. Loring & Associates* (mechanical/electrical). Lighting consultant: *Valley Lighting.* Landscape architects: *Wallace Roberts & Todd.* Photo murals: *Ashton Worthington.* General contractor and cost consultants: *The Whiting-Turner Contracting Company.*

Clemens Kalischer

LATH HOUSE, HERITAGE SQUARE
PHOENIX, ARIZONA
Robert R. Frankeberger

"A thriving, revitalized downtown could make a city out of our endless suburb . . . for no shopping center can emulate a downtown's sense of place, no branch office can pretend to be at the heart of matters," argues Phoenix architect Robert Frankeberger. Phoenix, like many of the newer, sprawling cities has suffered severe problems caused by decentralization of retail and office facilities. Toward this revitalization goal, and what may become its symbol, is the development through restoration and new construction of a small block, marked only as number 14 on the city maps, but known as the original townsite.

Called Heritage Square, this development could be the proving ground for a grander vision of converting what are now parking lots, vacant parcels of land, dilapidated buildings and a skid row known as "The Deuce" into a burgeoning cultural/historical/retail/office/residential complex in an area to the east and south of the central business district.

While the catalyst for Heritage Square is the restoration of the stately landmark Rosson House (bottom right), the centerpiece is the Lath House—an open-air pavilion to be used for outdoor concerts, arts and crafts shows, festivals, exhibits and convention events (for the convention center is only one block away). It is a remarkably appropriate architectural solution to the special problems of the hot Southwest climate, a new structure that relates in spirit to its historic neighbors,

and a space large enough to accommodate sizeable community events.

Covering about one-third of the block (see site plan opposite page) it took hundreds of Douglas fir poles and laminated wood beams to define a space that is 220 feet long, 80 feet wide and 23,200 square feet (with the inclusion of a block of meeting rooms). A latticework of laths filters sunlight, yet allows air to circulate, thereby creating a microclimate that is an immediately noticeable relief from the harsh sun.

Frankeberger was inspired in part by Bertram Goodhue's Conservatory in San Diego's Balboa Park, but he was also mindful of other buildings on the site in scale and proportions. The two-story-high structure maintains the same eave-to-ridge line height of the bungalows on the block, and the roof curvature softens its mass. Opening along an arcade, which surrounds the structure and is reminiscent of those once found along most business fronts in downtown, are large arched entrances.

The plan of the Lath House is broken into two segments—the grand expanse which links to a greenhouse under skylights (not fully developed yet), and an enclosed set of meeting rooms and back-up facilities. The floor is brick, set in 10-foot-square grid patterns. Lighting for evening events is by industrial-type fixtures in the Lath House, and period-piece light standards throughout the grounds of the Square.

Since Phoenix is short on historical build-

art of a scheme to continue revitalization of downtown Phoenix is the development—through restoration, rehabilitation and new construction—of block now called Heritage quare (see site plan). Because he Rosson House (left) stands n the original townsite, and s noteworthy quality, it has een restored and is used for museum and meeting rooms. Other neighboring residences re being converted into museum and office space. The ew construction on the site is grand, new open-air pavilion alled the Lath House (above, op left and overleaf). This wood-framed structure can be sed for a variety of public nd private events, day and ight, and has already been he location of a Chapter party or the Central Arizona/AIA. he Square received landmark tatus in 1976. Monroe Grade chool across the street from he Lath House (also seen in ite plan) is being considered or an art center.

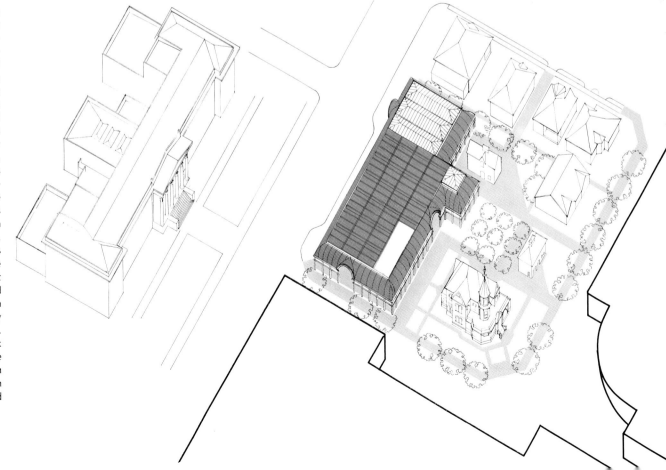

ings the restoration of the Rosson House is particularly noteworthy. Built in 1894 for Dr. Roland L. Rosson, it was designed by architect Alexander P. Petit in Queen Anne style with Eastlake ornamentation. In 1972 it was placed on the National Historic Register of Places. The house was fully restored after that by Frankeberger and a team of architect-volunteers as a local AIA Chapter project. It is now used as a museum and meeting center.

Several other houses on the site—the Silva House, the Teeter house, and two others called Stevens-Haustgen houses, a 1920's duplex and a carriage house—were respected in the plan. The Teeter and Stevens-Haustgen houses are being rehabilitated by Gerald A. Doyle and Associates. These bungalows are all small scale and represent a mix of styles ranging from the California "arts and crafts" movement to revivals of various other periods. They will house civic and community organizations including the headquarters of the Central Arizona Chapter of the AIA, the Historical Society, and a museum for the Salt River Project.

While the city still retains ownership of Block 14, the money for restoration of the Rosson House and other historic structures on the site, and the design work of the Lath House came from private donations, and Federal funding from a grant of the public works program of the Economic Development Administration, and a Department of the Interior Grant-in-Aid for Historic Preservation.

While Frankeberger was a member of the Rosson House restoration committee, he became so intrigued with the area's potential that he developed a comprehensive area plan. As he said, "One can't plan in a vacuum. I see this whole area as a unit." The development would include expanding the nearby Civic Plaza by adding 40,000 square feet of exhibition space, a 400-seat and a 1,200-seat theater, construction of a Mexican Mercado (arts and crafts center), adding other shops and businesses and perhaps a hotel, reviving a trolley line which ran through the area, and providing underground parking. Also included is a proposal to turn part of the Phoenix Union High School (a campus-like neo-classical set of buildings nearby) into a community college for the performing arts, and Monroe Grade School into an arts center.

The success of the revitalization of downtown Phoenix will, of course, depend on the proper orchestration of all the complex elements, but the wonderful and viable Heritage Square development should be regarded as one of Phoenix' finest center-city advances in that direction.

LATH HOUSE AT HERITAGE SQUARE, Phoenix, Arizona. Owner: *City of Phoenix.* Architect: *Robert R. Frankeberger.* Engineers: *Caruso Engineering Associates* (structural); *Lowry, Sorensen, Willcoxson Engineers* (electrical/mechanical). Landscape architect: *Jim Wheat.* General contractor: *J.R. Porter Construction Company.*

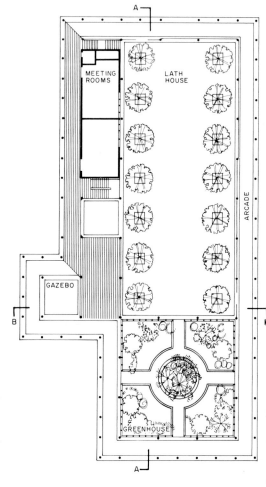

Receiving such plaudits as "a total delight" and "a fresh answer to community space" from the architectural jury which awarded the Lath House an Honor Award in 1980, the vast latticework structure defines and modulates the open arena (above and top left) and establishes a micro-climate which effectively combats the hot weather. Smaller enclosed meeting rooms were also included to diversify the usable space (see floor plan). A series of wood barn doors (as seen in the sections) can enclose the structure for security reasons, to shield street noise, and can be opened to facilitate moving exhibits in-and-out.

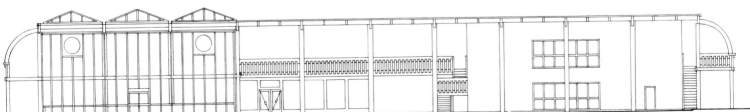

SECTION A-A

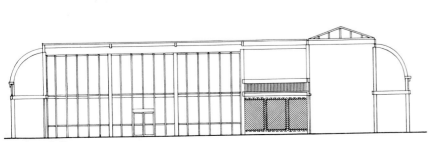

SECTION B-B

CITICORP CENTER NEW YORK CITY
Hugh Stubbins & Associates

Architects now working on the next generation of New York City skyscrapers should be paying close attention to Citicorp. Designed by Hugh Stubbins & Associates, it is the best of the newer office towers in the city as of now. You don't have to like its top—a lot of people think it's arbitrary. You may not like its skin—some people question a shining building in a matte city. But you have to like the base. The church, plaza and galleria at the ground level of Citicorp form a truly humane space which actually *invites* ordinary people to use it, offering them such small pleasures as comfortable places to meet and sit and bring their own food. It is not necessary to have money to spend to enjoy the public spaces of Citicorp; and depending on the time of day you see a sprinkling of older people relaxing at tables in the tree-filled, skylit atrium. And the church is there for quiet meditation.

Think of the plazas of the skyscrapers of the past decade, each empty except for its single correct, non-objective and non-objectionable sculpture of brightly colored bent steel—sensitively placed, of course. Think of the grudging, gloomy public space in other New York buildings—like the Galleria and Olympic Towers; public spaces put there by the owners in exchange for the profits to be made from higher floor area ratios granted by the City Planning Commission's incentive zoning program. Few citizens know that these empty concourses are supposed to be amenities, hard won by the Mayor's urban planners, for public enjoyment. But people know, because the architecture is inviting, that Citicorp is for them.

CITICORP CENTER, New York City. Owner: *Citibank/Citicorp.* Architects: *Hugh Stubbins and Associates, Inc.—principal architect: Hugh Stubbins; project architect: W. Easley Hammer; production architect: Howard E. Goldstein.* Associated architects: *Emery Roth and Sons.* Consultants: *LeMessurier Associates/SCI and the Office of James Ruderman (structural and foundations); Joseph R. Loring & Associates (mechanical/electrical and lighting of office space); Sasaki Associates (landscape); Vignelli Associates (graphics and design of church furniture and fittings).* Construction manager: *HRH Construction Corporation.*

Norman McGrath photos

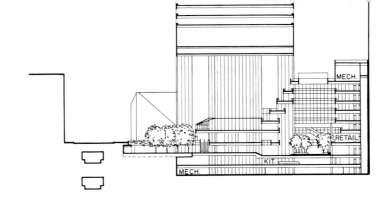

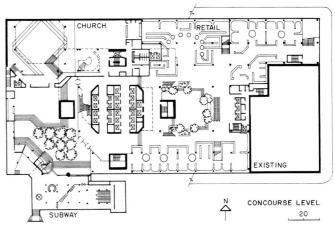

N △ CONCOURSE LEVEL
20

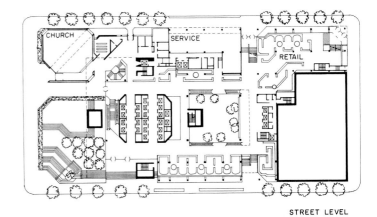

STREET LEVEL

The street environment of Citicorp Center is a triumph of urban design—the first project influenced and helped to fruition by the Mayor's Office of Midtown Planning that demonstrates convincingly what the Planning Commission's Urban Design Group has been trying to accomplish since its founding by former Mayor John V. Lindsay in 1967.

Credit belongs to Hugh Stubbins and his team, who from the beginning wanted to design a skyscraper which would relate to the street in a humane way; and to Reverend Dr. Ralph E. Peterson, pastor of the church rebuilt on the site, who also insisted that Citicorp Center provide ordinary citizens with places to meet, shop, eat and sit as well as worship. The top management of Citicorp, fortunately, were determined to meet their obligation to give the city fair return of handsome usable public space for the right to build at a floor area ratio of 18. The skylit galleria (opposite page and above) is open to the public who may bring their own food to the tables shown, or patronize the food shops adjacent to the court. There are several good restaurants and shops within the galleria (below). Office landscaping (right bottom) is used on typical tower floors.

George Czerna

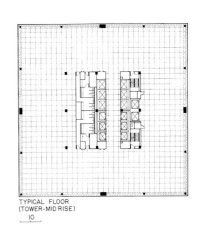

TYPICAL FLOOR
(TOWER-MID RISE)
10

George Czerna

George Czerna

George Czerna

Like buildings of many types, athletic facilities are being called upon to answer a constantly increasing list of specialized needs, each space often serving more than one function through flexible planning. The projects on the following pages form a particularly varied group of the results of such concerns.

The first project, a court tennis building at the Newport Casino, is the reconstruction (directed by Forbes Hailey Jeas Erneman) of an historic structure designed for a very esoteric game which requires very unusual facilities. It is at once the most specialized and the least flexible project in this chapter.

Carrying on the popular trend of recycling older buildings by adapting them to new uses, both the Back Bay Racquet Club in Boston (by Payette Associates and Graham/Meus) and Asphalt Green (by Total Environment Action) in New York are converted from buildings designed for different purposes — the former as an ink factory, the latter as an asphalt plant.

Despite general cutbacks in public spending, some ambitious youth centers continue to be built. Along with spaces for more passive pursuits, these contain extensive facilities for athletics. In addition to the reuse project of Asphalt Green, this chapter includes a strikingly modern center in Detroit by architects William Kessler and Associates and another in Newark by Ciardullo Ehmann. Both are particularly responsive to the desires of the young "clients," and the latter, St. Peter's Park, is especially noteworthy for making the most of very limited means.

At the opposite end of the spectrum of athletic facilities for the young are two gymnasiums for private schools: the Ainsworth Gymnasium at Smith College by The Architects Collaborative and the Mott Gymnasium at the Emma Willard School by Bohlin Powell Larkin Cywinski. In many respects, these demonstrate the same fiscal restraint required of the public facilities, although the accommodated activities may differ. As there is no one sport, there is no one athletic facility that meets all needs, and the following projects demonstrate some of the many possible varieties.

Chapter Six

Athletic Facilities

COURT TENNIS FACILITY
NEWPORT, RHODE ISLAND
Restored by
Forbes Hailey Jeas Erneman

There is a story that has long circulated through the narrow ranks of the world's court tennis players. It tells of a ranking lawn tennis player introduced to court tennis for the first time. His face flushed and brimming with excitement, he played for more than an hour. When play was over, the story goes, he turned to his hosts to pronounce his verdict. "What a wonderful game! Astonishing! Thrilling! Superb! . . . Who won?"

His question grew out of the game's all but impenetrable scoring system, but it was rhetorical for another reason. Nobody playing this ancient and delightfully arcane game for the first time wins. Even players who are adept in other racquet sports have noticeable difficulty coming to terms with the fundamental equipment of this game: a high net with a melancholy droop at its center, a racquet that looks and feels like something backed over

Paul Ferrino photos

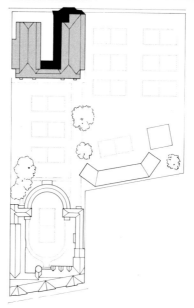

by a truck, and a ball covered in felt, over an inner winding of cloth and twine, that appears to have been fashioned in a kindergarten class—and only after considerable struggle.

These things, together with the cryptic scoring system and a court of hauntingly complex geometry, belong to the game's venerable beginnings. Older by far than lawn tennis, platform tennis, table tennis, squash racquets, or badminton—older in fact than all these combined—court tennis traces its origins to the twelfth century and to the cloistered abbeys of southwest France. From here the game spread rapidly to the rest of France, then across the Channel to England. The sixteenth century, a time of thralldom or even decline for most sports, was for court tennis a golden age. The game was played with a devotion that approached frenzy by the kings

of both England and France, and it became known, variously, as *royal tennis* or *real tennis*, names that it still bears today in other countries. In many of its essentials, the game has changed but little since the time of Henry VIII, for the court he built at Hampton Court (A.D. 1530) still stands, still reverberates with the sound of play, and, until surprisingly recently, still served as a model for new facilities.

But new court tennis facilities have risen grotesquely in cost since Henry's time. Once there may have been as many as 1800 courts in France alone. Today, only 30 playable courts remain in all the world. Around each is clustered a small nucleus of players so ardent, so loyal, so dedicated to the preservation of their game that the creation of a new court or—better still—the restoration of an old court, is attended by all the anticipation and

excitement of a royal birth.

Just such an event occurred in 1980 at the Newport Casino in Rhode Island. Amid the easy elegance of McKim, Mead and White's gracious, shingle-style enclosure, a court tennis facility badly damaged by fire in 1945 was painstakingly and beautifully restored. It was the first "new" court put into play in this country since 1923, and already many of the best players from around the world have come to test its excellence. The architect for this restoration was Peter Forbes, principal in the Boston firm of Forbes Hailey Jeas & Erneman. Forbes is himself a court tennis player, so he brought to the rebuilding task an invaluable first-hand knowledge of the game's requirements, as well as a deep respect for its traditions. The results more than justify Forbes's selection.

The new competition floor at Newport is

a rectangular, terra-cotta colored slab 31 by 93 feet on a side. By ancient custom, a sagging net divides the court into a server's side and a *hazard* (or receiver's) *side.* An assortment of wall openings and projections distinguish the two, giving each side an unmistakable identity. The most conspicuous of these, in the nomenclature of court tennis, is the *tambour,* a full-height thickening in the main wall near the rear of the *hazard side* (see plan). Today the *tambour* has no structural purpose whatever. It is merely an architectural remembrance of a medieval buttress or pilaster, but its chamfered edge is capable of producing unexpected (and indescribably irritating) caroms during play. Overhead, at a height of seven feet, the three other walls break back and up at about 40 degrees to form the *penthouse* (see section). This is the vestigial cloister roof. It is brought into play

during the serve in which the ball is gently lofted up to its canted, hardwood surface where it bounces along until it falls back to the floor on the *hazard side.* Play is then joined. The two long walls are playable to a height of 18 feet; the end walls to 24 feet. The ceiling, if any, is out of bounds. Play across the net is fast, tactics and shot selection are important, and court position is crucial. The server defends the wall opening at his back called the *dedans.* A similar but smaller opening at the back of the receiver is the *grille.* Some say that in medieval times these two openings were developed as pass-throughs so that thirsty players might be refreshed quickly. Today their function is simple: drive a ball through either opening and the point is over. The fourth wall, the long wall under the *penthouse,* is marked by a series of closely spaced openings called the

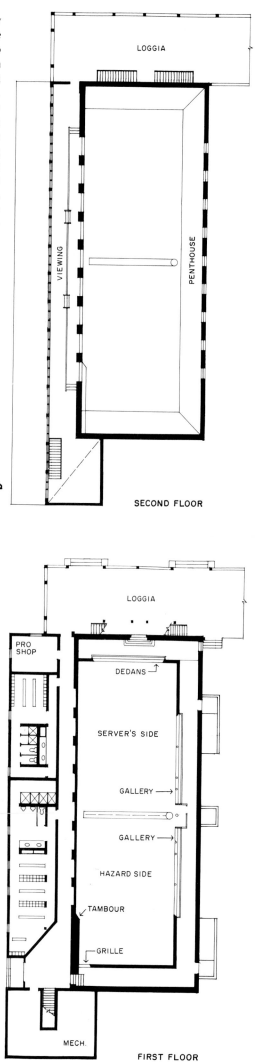

SECOND FLOOR

LOGGIA

VIEWING

PENTHOUSE

LOGGIA

PRO SHOP

DEDANS →

SERVER'S SIDE

GALLERY →

GALLERY →

HAZARD SIDE

↘ TAMBOUR

↳ GRILLE

MECH.

FIRST FLOOR

Because the ball is white, the colors of the competition surfaces must be selected to form a suitably contrasting background. Experiments over several centuries with a variety of colors led to the gradual preference of dull red for floor and slate gray for walls. The gray tone cannot be achieved using familiar plaster additives like lamp black, because carbon

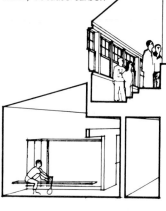

products tend to come off on the ball. Manganese dioxide is used to tone the walls at Newport. Black is used for most of the floor markings (chase lines), red for boundaries of play, and blue for the bandeau, *the line that marks the edge of the penthouse.*

gallery. Each opening is identified. A ball struck into the *winning gallery* (that is the second gallery on the *hazard side*) is an outright winner. A ball that bounced twice in play, or a ball driven into any of the other gallery openings results in a *chase*. This is a scoring device that places a point in escrow, but a device so convoluted, so excruciatingly complex when first encountered that it is best left undescribed—except to note that it is the device by which the serve changes from one player to another.

Tambour, penthouse, dedans, grille, gallery, chase. . . .Confusing? You bet. They have confused novice players for centuries. But they are the distinguishing features of a game that is fun to play, a game that makes captivating theater, a game that is played in a setting as medieval in character as any Romanesque cathedral.

The task of re-creating this setting at Newport was made no easier by the absence of accurate records. Forbes worked from old photographs that showed the original 1880 structure, designed by Boston architects R.G. and G.R. Shaw, before it was ravaged by fire. He got important assistance from court tennis veterans and, because the Casino is on the National Register of Historic Places, from several quasi-public bodies including the Rhode Island Historical Commission. It was the hope of all concerned that the building's exteriors could be reproduced with reasonable fidelity to the original. Though some changes were unavoidable (see comparative photos below right) the final result is a very plausible facsimile that disappoints no one. Substantial changes were made within. Steel trusses replace the heavy timber originals, and steel pipe columns buried in the wall now carry the

roof loads down to the foundations. To augment light from the clerestories, and to make night play possible, Forbes designed a catwalk that runs over the center of the court down its long axis. High-intensity metal halide fixtures are mounted on the catwalk on two-foot centers. Turned upward, they flood the court below with pleasant, indirect light that reaches about 100 footcandles at the net.

The competition surfaces were a special challenge. A very hard cement plaster was needed, a plaster that could withstand the constant abrasions and impacts of play, yet could be applied across very broad surfaces without seams or control joints of any kind. Research seemed to suggest that the most promising product was "Bickley's cement," a "sweatless," somewhat mysterious substance used with notable success at several earlier courts in England and America, and named

after its itinerant, long-deceased, inventor Joseph Bickley. Bickley had patented the product but, either by accident or by design, he had omitted at least two critical ingredients from the formula he had supplied to the Patent Office. Had Bickley taken his secret formula to the grave? Perhaps. But when the first tests at Newport with the Patent Office formula produced nothing but desultory results, Forbes sought help. He found it at the Edward Walsh Company in the person of Robert Evans, third-generation Yankee plasterer, and a man who quite evidently liked a challenge. After many trials with different additives, Evans produced a material so close in appearance and behavior to Bickley's that the two materials are virtually indistinguishable. It is the Evans material, under an epoxy sealer, that covers the almost 8,000 square feet of competition surfaces at Newport.

This rebuilding effort is independent of, but coincidental with, an ongoing $2 million program to restore the Newport Casino. Work has been completed on the McKim, Mead and White facade that lines Bellevue Avenue as well as on the Horseshoe Piazza. The grandstand around the central lawn tennis court has been restored, and more work on other casino facilities will follow as funds become available.

The rebuilding of this extraordinary structure cost about $420,000 including all fees. The work was undertaken on the initiative of The United States Court Tennis Association (John E. Slater, president) and for the express purpose of creating a "national court": a court on which any American can play as his birthright. It is, in this way, the only public court tennis facility in the United States.

No one need worry that any of this new work will threaten either the beauty of individual structures or the aura of a vanished age that clings to the Casino in all its parts. These things are tenaciously preserved. In one instance, these continuities have even been extended by a reforged link to an even more distant past. For in the high-ceilinged central chamber of the court tennis facility, Henry VIII could toss off his cloak and coronet, grab a racquet, and pick up just about where he left off.

COURT TENNIS FACILITY, Newport. Owners: *United States Court Tennis Association and the International Tennis Hall of Fame.* Architects: *Forbes Hailey Jeas Erneman.* Engineers: *Keefe and Regan* (structural); *M. L. Dee and Associates* (mechanical). Contractor: *Walsh Brothers, Incorporated.*

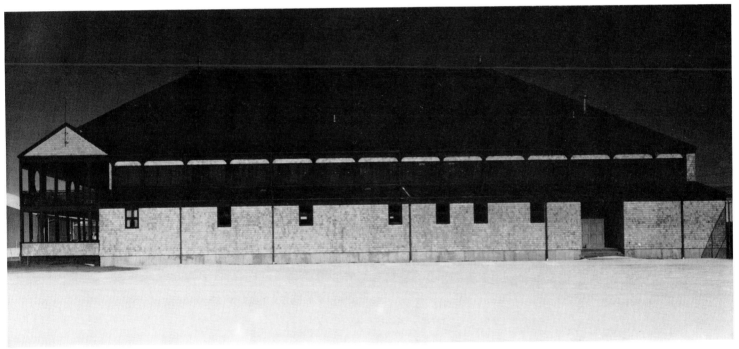

Comparative photographs, taken three-quarters of a century apart, show the east facades of the old and new structures. The upper level gallery, then and now, served as a raised viewing platform for both court tennis (photo far left) and lawn tennis (photo left) on the outdoor field courts. Photos, far left, show the new dressing rooms.

Paul Ferrino photos

BACK BAY RACQUET CLUB BOSTON, MASSACHUSETTS
Payette Associates & Graham/Meus

Racquetball, the upstart of American racquet sports, has found a proper Bostonian home in a converted ink factory. Ideally situated in the city's affluent Back Bay, the 90-year-old building was nearly vacant when architect and racquetball enthusiast Gary Graham perceived its hidden potential: the bay spacing of the five-story cast-iron and timber frame structure was exactly the right gauge to accommodate twelve 20- by 40-foot regulation-size courts. Market analysis convinced a group of developers that Boston's first racquetball installation would turn a handsome profit, especially if its appeal were broadened with full health-center facilities. The completed project is a joint-venture design by Payette Associates and Graham/Meus. Every detail of the vintage facade has been preserved except for a wooden storefront (see "before" photo, near left), which the architects considered awkwardly underscaled. Robust new columns frame butt-glazed windows that give passers-by a look into the pro shop (open to the public) and beyond to a glass-walled racquetball court. "Since this is an unabashedly commercial venture, we felt we ought to put the game itself on display," says Gary Graham. Inside the entrance, the transformation of the factory is declared no less emphatically by angled walls that slice through the regular grid of cast-iron columns. Racquetball is played in courts with back walls of clear tempered glass. Because the factory lofts were too low to house these 20-foot-high cubicals, original floors were removed. By staggering new split-level tiers on either side of central galleries (section overleaf), the architects have given spectators a choice of vantage points from which to follow the fast-paced action.

BACK BAY RACQUET CLUB, Boston, Massachusetts. Owner: *Boston Racquetball Associates.* Architects: *Payette Associates, Inc.-Graham/Meus Inc.— Gary Graham and Daniel Meus, architects-in-charge; Robert Quijano, James Pierce, designers-draftsmen.* Engineers: *Simpson Gumpertz & Heger* (structural), *Shooshanian Engineering* (mechanical). Graphics consultants: *Coco Raynes/Graphics Inc.* Contractor: *Henry E. Wile Corp.*

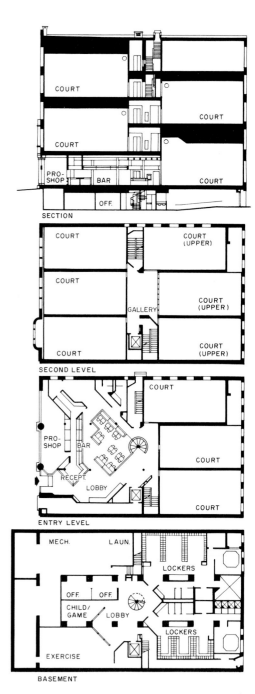

SECTION

COURT
COURT
COURT
PRO-SHOP   BAR   COURT
OFF.

SECOND LEVEL

COURT
COURT
COURT (UPPER)
COURT (UPPER)
COURT (UPPER)
GALLERY
COURT

ENTRY LEVEL

PRO-SHOP   BAR
RECEPT.
LOBBY
COURT
COURT
COURT

BASEMENT

MECH.   LAUN.
LOCKERS
OFF.   OFF.
CHILD/GAME   LOBBY
LOCKERS
EXERCISE

Through a stroke of serendipity, the original cast-iron and timber supports of an old Carter's Ink factory were found to have the right dimensions—in plan—for standard racquetball courts. These white cubicles—20 feet wide, 40 feet long, and 20 feet high—were constructed of particle board faced with plastic laminate, clipped to light steel studs. Unfortunately, extant ceilings were too low, and the necessary removal of floors threatened the stability of columnar pin connections. In order to stiffen the connections without extending reinforcement beyond court walls, the architects placed steel plates on either side of the joints, capped them at bottom and sides, and poured concrete between them.

In the lobby and lounge (right), the grid imposed by this post-and-beam structure is dramatically twisted 45 degrees. Besides focusing one's view toward a showcase racquetball court—and the restaurant bar—these diagonal planes channel circulation down a winding stair to the basement lockers, exercise room, and children's play area. The architects describe their dynamic shift of geometry as "a not-so-subtle analogy to the movement of the game itself," a theme that is echoed in the horizontal lines of street-level graphics and interior trim. Visible woodwork is maple, the preferred material for racquetball court floors.

YOUNG RECREATION CENTER
DETROIT, MICHIGAN
William Kessler & Associates

©Timothy Hursley/B. Korab, Ltd. photos

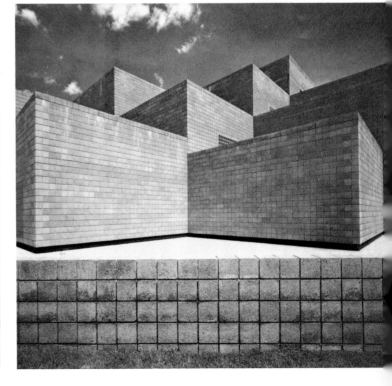

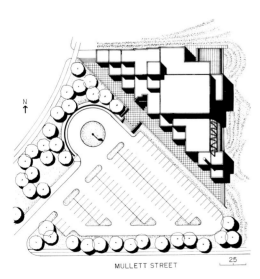

MULLETT STREET

25

The completion of Detroit's $4-million Coleman A. Young Recreation Center marks one of the last phases of a sweeping urban renewal program that began in 1954 when the city bulldozed 129 acres of slums known as the Black Bottom. Rechristened Elmwood, this area has become a patchwork of parks and mixed-income housing. The recreation center, which is named after the city's incumbent mayor, was designed to give Elmwood a much-needed focus for community life. Architects William Kessler & Associates have created a durable, low-maintenance structure with a distinctly urban blend of toughness and glamour. The stepped geometry of the entrance facade expresses a modular composition that governs every element of the building, from the eight-inch blocks of glass and ground-face concrete that clad both exterior and interior to the 24-foot grid of the triangular plan. Two stories are organized compactly into three principal zones of activity: senior citizens' arts and crafts workshops, multi-use community areas, and athletic facilities. For the most part, materials and colors form a quiet backdrop to human activity, although there is unrestrained drama in the virtuoso display of glass block in columns softly lit from within, shimmering screen walls, and translucent vaults over the boxing ring and swimming pool. As a precaution against vandalism, exterior glazing is generally confined to upper portions of the building. Of course, the best protection is the enthusiastic involvement of Elmwood residents, whose District Council maintains offices just off the lobby. Mayor Young could not have asked for a better namesake, or more tangible evidence that Detroit's long-promised renaissance is still within reach.

COLEMAN A. YOUNG RECREATION CENTER, Detroit, Michigan. Owner: *City of Detroit.* Architects: *William Kessler and Associates, Inc.* —*Edward Francis, FAIA, principal-in-charge; James Cardoza, AIA, Michael Patten, AIA, project design; Richard Adelson, Tom Paczkowski, AIA, Eugene DiLaura, FAIA, project execution.* Engineers: *McClurg Associates* (structural), *Hoyem-Basso* (mechanical, electrical, civil). General contractor: *J.A. Ferguson.*

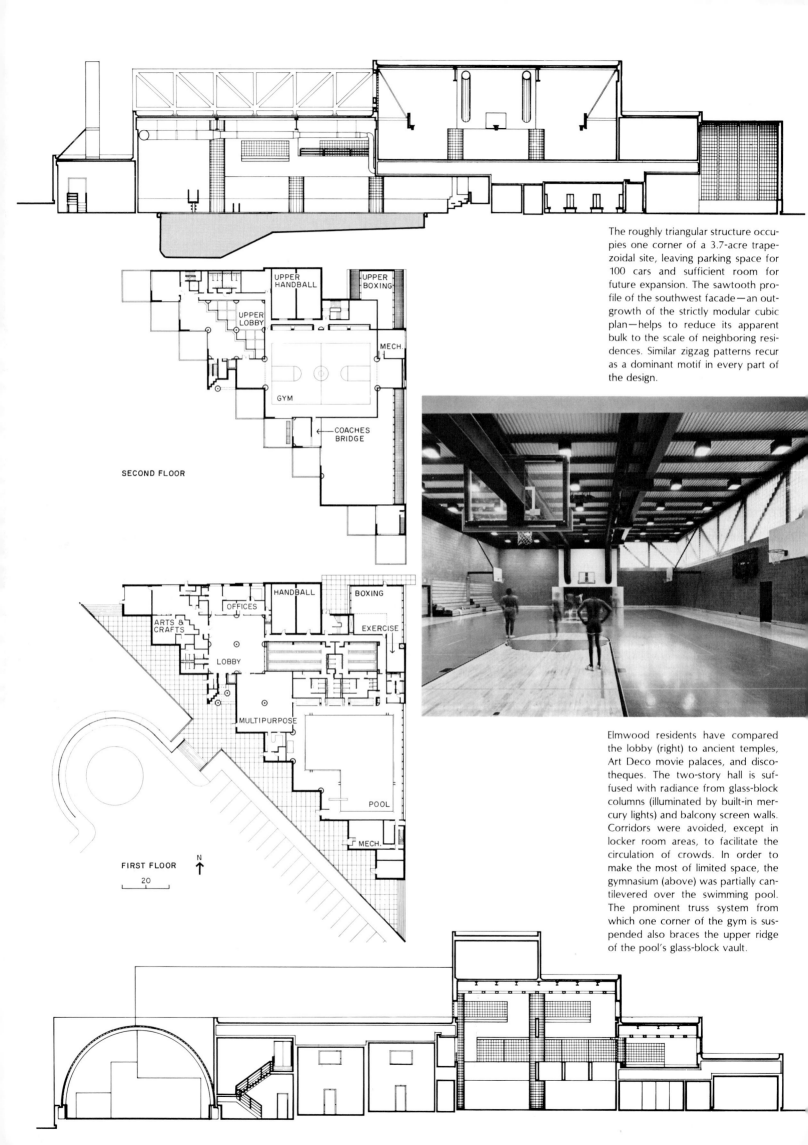

The roughly triangular structure occupies one corner of a 3.7-acre trapezoidal site, leaving parking space for 100 cars and sufficient room for future expansion. The sawtooth profile of the southwest facade—an outgrowth of the strictly modular cubic plan—helps to reduce its apparent bulk to the scale of neighboring residences. Similar zigzag patterns recur as a dominant motif in every part of the design.

UPPER HANDBALL
UPPER BOXING
UPPER LOBBY
MECH.
GYM
COACHES BRIDGE

SECOND FLOOR

ARTS & CRAFTS
OFFICES
HANDBALL
BOXING
EXERCISE
LOBBY
MULTIPURPOSE
POOL
MECH.

FIRST FLOOR
N
20

Elmwood residents have compared the lobby (right) to ancient temples, Art Deco movie palaces, and discotheques. The two-story hall is suffused with radiance from glass-block columns (illuminated by built-in mercury lights) and balcony screen walls. Corridors were avoided, except in locker room areas, to facilitate the circulation of crowds. In order to make the most of limited space, the gymnasium (above) was partially cantilevered over the swimming pool. The prominent truss system from which one corner of the gym is suspended also braces the upper ridge of the pool's glass-block vault.

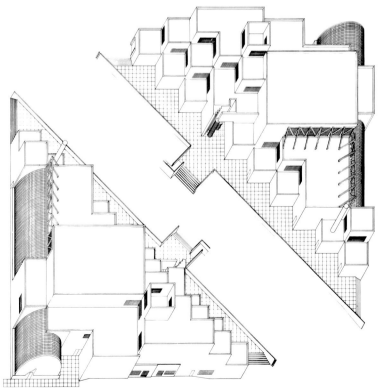

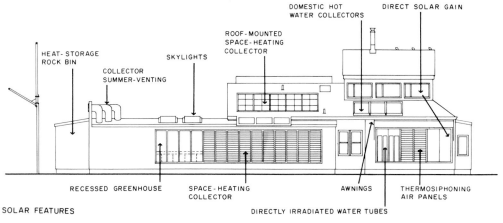

SOLAR FEATURES

HEAT-STORAGE ROCK BIN — COLLECTOR SUMMER-VENTING — SKYLIGHTS — ROOF-MOUNTED SPACE-HEATING COLLECTOR — DOMESTIC HOT WATER COLLECTORS — DIRECT SOLAR GAIN

RECESSED GREENHOUSE — SPACE-HEATING COLLECTOR — DIRECTLY IRRADIATED WATER TUBES — AWNINGS — THERMOSIPHONING AIR PANELS

Manhattan schoolchildren come from as far afield as Harlem and Chinatown to visit a recycled fireboat house (below) for "hands-on" experience of waterfront ecology. A site-fabricated solar collector system is part of a wide assortment of solar retrofit apparatus that keeps operating expenses down while demonstrating practical energy-conservation techniques. A sister project, the Asphalt Green Sports & Arts Center (opposite), is now being installed in a former asphalt plant across the street. A gym occupies the open space under a mammoth concrete vault.

Joseph W. Molitor

ASPHALT GREEN NEW YORK CITY
Total Environment Action

No arbitrary boundaries are drawn between recreation and education on the grounds of Asphalt Green, a 5¼-acre recycling project in New York City that combines the resources of a disused fireboat station (above left) and an abandoned municipal asphalt plant (opposite). This unlikely marriage of building types has been arranged by an enterprising consortium of city and state agencies, private benefactors, and grassroots community organizations. Once construction has been finished (work on the asphalt plant is still in progress), the complex will offer New Yorkers a formidable assemblage of cultural, athletic, and educational programs.

The asphalt plant—designed in the 1940s by Kahn & Jacobs and recently named an official city landmark for its pioneering structure of parabolic concrete vaults—will eventually house locker rooms and other sports facilities, an assembly hall, a little theater, art studio, and classrooms. The fireboat house, a half-century-old frame structure on a dock in the East River, is already being operated by the Board of Education as a marine biology

and energy study center for thousands of city school children.

It is doubtful that either building would have survived much longer without the foresight and dedication of the Neighborhood Committee for Asphalt Green, a group of Manhattan residents headed by Dr. George E. Murphy. At its own expense, the Committee graded and landscaped the site of the asphalt plant to supplement the meager playing fields of local public and private schools, and encouraged the formulation of new uses for the derelict buildings. In order to minimize life-cycle costs, it was decided that any renovation of this complex should be highly energy-efficient. With a grant from the New York State Energy Research and Development Authority, an exhaustive analysis was conducted by Total Environmental Action, Inc., who were also the architects for the fireboat house project. Joint architects for the asphalt plant were Hellmuth, Obata & Kassabaum and Pasanella + Klein.

Gas-driven generators for electric power are being installed in the asphalt plant. Heat

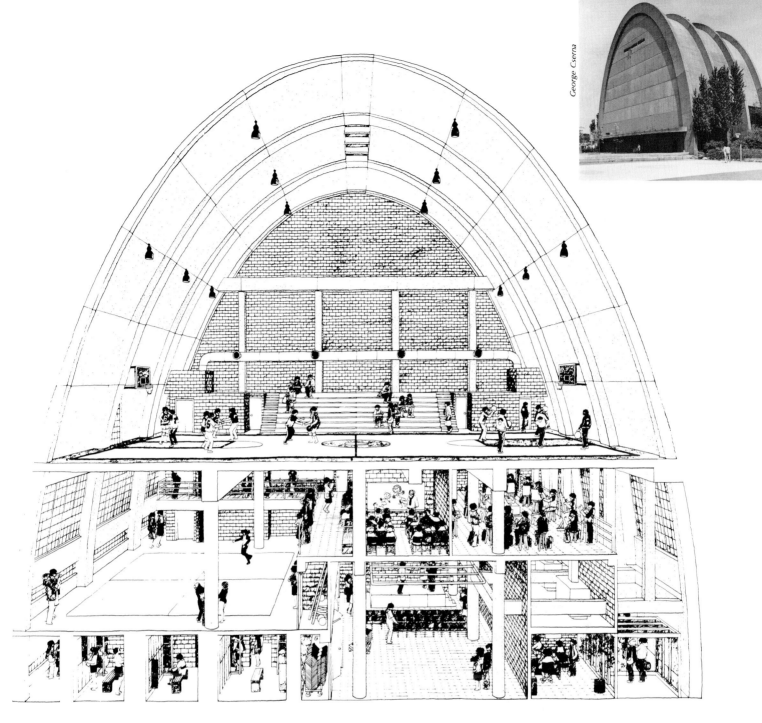

George Cserna

from the generators, lights, and building occupants will be recovered and conserved by heavy insulation of the concrete shell. Water will be chilled and stored during off-peak hours, and a wind turbine will eventually stand nearby on Mill Rock Island, where the Committee hopes to establish a small working farm. Total Environmental Action estimates that energy costs for the Sports and Arts Center will be roughly a third the amount needed for conventional systems.

The fireboat house has been outfitted with an array of active and passive solar devices that ought to cut heating costs 54 per cent (project manager Daniel Scully calls the south side of the building a "solar smorgasbord"—see elevation above left). Even though the 27-degree pitch of the first-story roof is shallower than the ideal angle for collectors at this latitude, the architects were eager to show the public that solar retrofit is readily adaptable on a modest scale to "imperfect" conditions, and that it can be an integral part of esthetically pleasing buildings. (The curved roof, vents, and smokestack

over new second-story offices were designed to enhance the building's nautical image.) For young visitors downstairs, a network of color-coded ducts, visible heat-storage water tanks, a photovoltaic cell, and a menagerie of tadpoles, fish, and crabs make science class an adventure.

ASPHALT GREEN, New York, New York. Owner: City of New York. FIREBOAT HOUSE. Architects: *Total Environmental Action, Inc.—Paul Pietz, project architect; Daniel Scully, project manager.* Associated architects: *Steven Robinson Associates— Steven Zalben, project manager.* Engineers: *Robert Silman Associates, PC* (structural), *John Dedyo* (sanitary), *Winslow Fuller* (solar). Contractor: *ABRA Construction Co.* SPORTS & ARTS CENTER. Architects: *Hellmuth, Obata & Kassabaum/Pasanella + Klein—J. Arvid Klein, Graeme A. Whitelaw, management; Harry S. Culpin, Giovanni Pasanella, design; Tom Stetz, project architect; Michele Lewis, designer.* Engineers: *Robert Silman Associates, PC; Sidney W. Barbanel, PC.* Consultants: *Total Environmental Action with Sidney Barbanel* (energy analysis). Contractor: *Series Contracting Corp.*

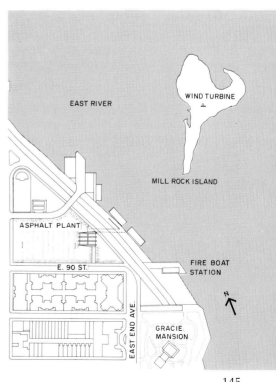

EAST RIVER

WIND TURBINE

MILL ROCK ISLAND

ASPHALT PLANT

E. 90 ST.

EAST END AVE.

FIRE BOAT STATION

GRACIE MANSION

N

John McNanie

ST. PETER'S PARK RECREATION CENTER
NEWARK, NEW JERSEY
Ciardullo Ehmann

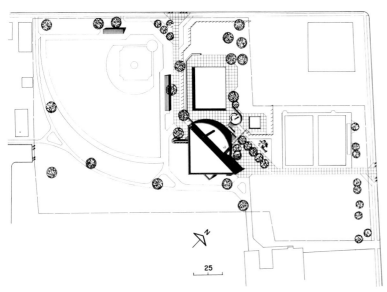

25

Interjecting facilities for the kind of lively involvement that keeps neighborhood youngsters alert and interested, this airy pavilion and large swimming pool occupy part of a more traditional park that once primarily catered to the sedate habits of strolling and sitting. The pavilion houses changing rooms and machinery for the pool—as well as offices and a large multiple-use space, overlooked by a balcony snack bar (see plans overleaf). The balcony extends out of the building to a large semi-circular terrace, where ventilation stacks from the changing rooms below have been bent into playful white sculptures.

The arrangement allows quieter pursuits at the second level, out of the heavy traffic to and from the changing rooms. A ramp to the second level projects from the building, and allows access for the handicapped. The long diagonal wall facing the pool is glazed with unusually large sheets of clear shatterproof plastic, allowing both views toward the pool and surveillance of indoor activities from two of the adjacent streets. The other two walls of brick are almost solid, shielding the sun from the south and supporting two sides of the steel roof structure.

After more than a year's use, the building remained almost as fresh and spotless as the day it opened, in a neighborhood where graffiti and vandalism are common. The architects attribute a large part of this

Nathaniel Lieberman

147

Nathaniel Lieberman

success to the sense of possession and pride that the users have in this new neighborhood focus. Accordingly, this project provides them with one of their greater sources of satisfaction and pleasure. It is also proof of their feeling about the importance of really getting to know the particular neighborhood in which a project is to be built—a crucial element in their design process.

In keeping with these particular architects' highly pragmatic design approach, Saint Peters is an interesting mix of practicality and playfulness. The combination of the triangle and the semicircular forms grew as much from a desire to reinforce natural circulation patterns and to create a meaningful relationship between pool and building, as it did from a desire for a fresh image. Similarly, the two-levels were the result of the need for a separation of different types of activities. And they were the result of a desire for interesting spatial relationships.

SAINT PETERS PARK RECREATION CENTER, Newark, New Jersey. Owner: *City of Newark*. Architects: *Ciardullo Ehmann—project architect: Paul Spears*. Engineers: *Environmental Engineering (soils); George Deng (air handling); Marian Swiechowski (plumbing, electrical, swimming pool)*. Landscape architect: *Miceli Weed Kulik*. Cost consultant: *Thomas Barrella*. General contractor: *Guasto Construction*.

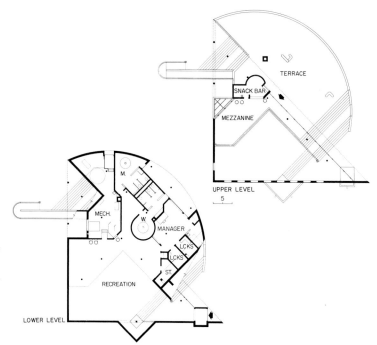

Nathaniel Lieberman

John McNanie photos except noted

Nathaniel Lieberman

AINSWORTH GYMNASIUM, SMITH COLLEGE NORTHAMPTON, MASSACHUSETTS
The Architects Collaborative

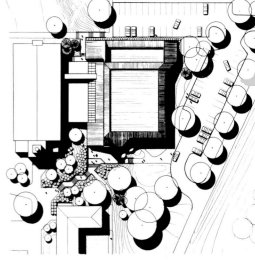

SITE PLAN

The physical health of the student body has been a vital concern of Smith College in Northampton, Massachusetts, from its founding in 1875. Just two years before, *Sex In Education*, written by the eminent physician Edward Hammond Clarke of Harvard College, admonished parents to spare their daughters the agonies of higher education—arguing that the demands of higher education could destroy a woman's ability to bear children by overtaxing her at a critical stage in her adolescent development.

The argument sounds patently ridiculous today. But many parents took Clark's words to heart. And pioneering women's colleges, including Smith, Vassar, and Wellesley, required students to take a certain number of hours of physical education just to reassure anxious parents.

The new Ainsworth Gymnasium at Smith, designed by The Architects Collaborative, is a striking example of how far this concern has matured. In the century since the founding of Smith and the completion of Ainsworth, women's college sports have developed from exercises to intramural recreation and intercollegiate competition.

As a modern physical education facility, Ainsworth comprises a full-sized gymnasium with spectator seating for 600, a 25-yard, six-lane swimming and diving pool with spectator seating for 300, six squash courts with spectator seating for 150 overlooking two courts, and locker, shower, and office space for students, staff, and faculty. As an addition to Smith's physical plant, Ainsworth enlarges

the capabilities of adjoining Scott Gymnasium, erected in 1923, while enhancing the attractiveness of both.

The need for a new gymnasium for Smith became clear by the mid-1960s, when then-president Thomas Mendenhall began a formal inquiry with TAC. Growing interest in women's sports had rendered Scott obsolete. Its pool, three lanes wide with a shallow visitors' balcony, had always seemed too narrow for such events as the school's traditional "Lifeguard Show," a water ballet and comedy staged during Parents Weekend and Commencement. The gymnasium too had been considered dark and confining because of its overhanging mezzanine gallery, which constituted the only spectator space. Nor could the few squash courts in the old Alumnae Gymnasium satisfy new recruits to this once male-dominated sport.

Working with the school's department of physical plant, TAC has created a compact, efficient, and logical solution that stresses easy movement within the two integrated gymnasiums near Smith's renowned playing fields, sports facilities that conform to contemporary regulations, generous provisions for spectators attending competitive events, and energy conservation—an important consideration in a voluminous four-story 52,000-square-foot space. School and designer dallied briefly with a more remote site. Concentration won out over dispersal for numerous reasons.

Scott was already located at the school's "back door," where the unavoidable bulk of

The circulation corridor that joins the new Ainsworth Gym to the older Scott Gym to its east dominates these views of the north facade. Rising beside the trapezoidal opening is the north stair tower.

©Nick Wheeler photos

the new building would least encroach on the open space of this bucolic campus of residential "houses" and classroom buildings. Consequently, Ainsworth could share Scott's precious parking area. Walking distance between different sporting events could also be saved. Perhaps most important of all, merging Ainsworth and Scott made possible the modernization of Scott's outmoded interiors, as well as the elimination of redundant facilities.

The genius of the resulting design is its circulation. To quote David G. Sheffield, one of two partners-in-charge at TAC with John C. Harkness, "Circulation is the only area in a gymnasium where you can be creative. The rest is set by sports regulations."

A low pavilion housing that Scott swimming pool became the logical dividing line between old and new. Originally slated for demolition, this masonry structure impressed TAC with its graceful vaulted ceiling. TAC converted it into a lounge, pierced its glazed walls with doorways, and ran an enclosed multi-level "street" beside it as the principal circulation corridor for both buildings. Besides providing access to all four levels of the new building, the corridor connects directly to two of Scott's three levels.

Finding your way in Ainsworth is greatly facilitated by the many visual cues that line this passage. Each level has its own distinct character. The basement level is below grade, and runs strictly within the space joining pool, women's and men's lockers, and squash courts. At the ground-floor level, the elevation rises past the second-level balcony

and third-level fascia to a sloping skylighted ceiling three stories high.

Primary color is liberally applied throughout, emphasizing the strongly industrial character of the building by articulating its component parts. The pipe railings that line the second-level gallery and the rafters carrying the skylights from the third-level fascia of Ainsworth to the cornice of Scott are painted yellow. The ground-floor security booth, office doors and window frames, and overhead air duct are blue. Second-level doors and window frames and new doors and trophy cases in Scott's window openings are red. The informal color scheme is consistently applied in the other interior spaces of both buildings.

Each sport expresses its own character nevertheless. The natatorium, whose six-lane 25-yard-long pool conforms to NCAA standards, is a serene study in white tile walls with blue tile seating coves for poolside use. Direct outdoor lighting is not permitted to reach the pool since glare can confuse swimmers and cause accidents. However, outdoor light is permitted to spill indirectly into the large (70 feet by 103 feet by 27 feet high) room by way of windows fronting the second-level gallery and a slanting clerestory window band on the opposite wall.

Yellow trusses threaded by blue air ducts generate a sense of drama in the airy (96 feet by 108 feet by 26 feet high) third-level gymnasium. The views from the almost windowless room are surprisingly rewarding—a projecting bay window at the north stair tower

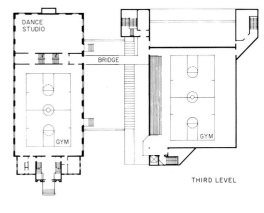

THIRD LEVEL

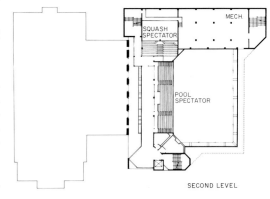

SECOND LEVEL

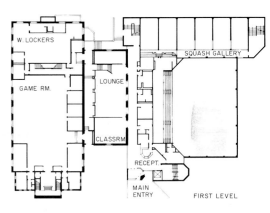

FIRST LEVEL

BASEMENT

As plans and section show, the two buildings join at two levels: through the lounge shown at left and on the bridge visible in the circulation corridor shown at right. Banners represent important Smith sports, years founded, and class colors for years.

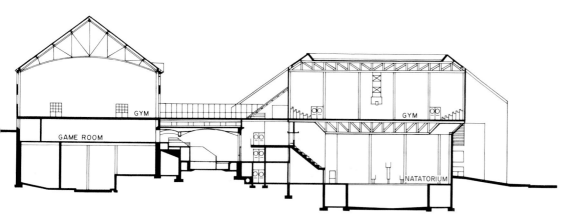

looks down to the indoor "street." A bridge at the south stair carries pedestrians from this gymnasium to its newly renovated counterpart in Scott.

There is palpable tension in the design for the squash courts, perhaps owing in part to the constraints of the game—small (18 feet 6 inches by 32 feet by 16 feet high) court size, use of four walls for play, and difficulty of viewing the game from any vantage point but above court. The design creates considerable excitement here while exercising strictest economy. The intersection of concrete encased columns and beams, block-wall infill, and plaster court walls, traversed by oversized ducts and a narrow teaching gallery, produces the same restless shifting and sliding suggestive of historic styles like De Stijl.

Quite a different temperament is manifest in the lounge fashioned from the Scott natatorium. Where sports facilities are stripped to bare structure and surfaces left hard and often impervious, the lounge responds with carpeting, rounded foam sectional seating, and, in the raised balcony where limited food service is available, pedestal chairs and tables in the Saarinen tradition.

This is a most workable building, to judge from the comments of school officials. Maintenance is uncomplicated, thanks to the abundant use of ceramic tile, exposed block, and polyurethane coatings over oak plank and concrete slab. Circulation is straightforward; users consult the directory map—here a *section* rather than a *floor plan,* just once or twice to understand how the building works.

Energy consumption, based on forced hot air using heat exchangers and steam supplied by the campus central steam plant, is minimized by a highly effective (70 per cent) air to air heat exchanger that preheats fresh air with heat transferred from exhaust air via aluminum plates. (The engineer's estimated payback period for the exchanger was less than two years.)

Ainsworth is also a good neighbor. To blunt the visual impact of its 154 feet (east-west axis) by 172 feet (north-south axis) by 72 feet (pool deck to parapet), TAC stopped the brick facing common to virtually all campus buildings at the second floor spandrel. Above steel siding painted a dark brown has been applied over the steel frame. The angular facade gestures to New England vernacular.

Smith College has wasted no time assimilating Ainsworth Gymnasium and the renovated Scott Gymnasium into campus life. The buildings are busy during the school year from 7 A.M. to 10 P.M.

AINSWORTH GYMNASIUM, Northampton, Massachusetts. Owner: *Smith College.* Architects: *The Architects Collaborative—David G. Sheffield, John C. Harkness, principals-in-charge; James Armstrong, project architect; Mark Hammer, Toby Sirois, architectural team; Sherry Caplan, interior designer; Chuck Gibson, graphic designer; Laurence Zuelke, Terry Jacoby, landscape; Bill Robinson, supervision; Ronald Chiaramonte, specifications.* Engineers: *Souza & True* (structural); *Van Zelm, Heywood and Shadford* (mechanical/electrical). General contractor: *Aquadro & Cerrutti.*

Each sport receives individual interior treatment, including swimming at left, basketball and other gymnastics at right, and squash, above. The top view is of the bay window in the gym, which overlooks indoor "street."

Joseph W. Molitor photos

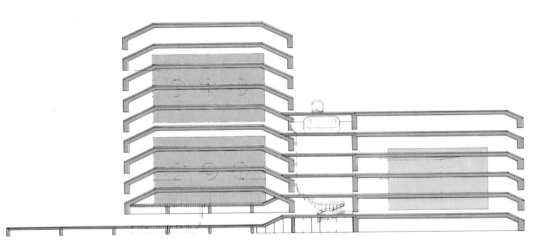

MOTT GYMNASIUM, EMMA WILLARD SCHOOL TROY, NEW YORK
Bohlin Powell Larkin Cywinski

Ivy-covered halls built in the early years of this century border the playing fields and tennis courts of the Emma Willard School, a private academy for girls in Troy, New York. In designing a new multi-purpose gymnasium next to the school's main quadrangle, architects Bohlin Powell Larkin Cywinski took pains to honor campus traditions while allowing for future growth. The structure shown above represents the initial phase of a two-stage project which will ultimately include an indoor swimming pool (see axonometric above). A tight budget necessitated simple forms and materials throughout. The gym is essentially a large shed, spanned by precast concrete beams. Notched piers at the eastern end (opposite above) indicate where roof members for the projected pool will rest. Although varsity competitions and community events are held here occasionally, the building is primarily devoted to intramural athletics and physical education. The gym can be subdivided into two tennis courts, two basketball courts, two volleyball courts, or any desired combination of playing areas. It is

also an ideal setting for gymnastics. Daylight enters through insulated fiberglass panels set into the north wall. Faculty offices and a mezzanine receive natural illumination from a glazed two-story lobby, which will be shaded during the warm months by a red steel trellis planted with vines. A pergola relieves the blank expanse of the southern gable wall, whose subtly varied concrete surfaces echo the texture and color of ashlar masonry in the old quad and in a library and arts building designed by Edward Larrabee Barnes. Roofs are covered with zinc-alloy that will weather to the tone of slate. Ivy, the sine qua non for campus landmarks, has already begun to climb the south facade.

CHARLES STEWART MOTT GYMNASIUM, The Emma Willard School, Troy, New York. Owner: *The Emma Willard School.* Architects: *Bohlin Powell Larkin Cywinski—Peter Q. Bohlin, FAIA, partner-in-charge; Jon C. Jackson, AIA, project architect.* Engineers: *Josep Firnkas* (structural), *Frederick Sheldon* (mechanical), *Gordon Wimmer* (electrical). General contractor: *Cassabone Brothers, Inc.*

As the plan and axonometric indicate, the precast concrete structure of the gymnasium will eventually be extended to enclose a swimming pool. The mezzanine (lower right) that overlooks the gym will also have a view of the pool, providing a grandstand for spectators and a convenient waiting area and instructional/social space. Only minimal locker room facilities were planned because most Emma Willard students prefer to change in their own rooms.

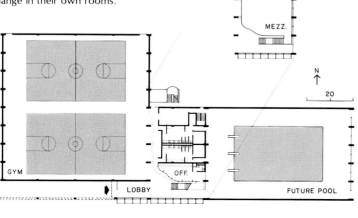

MEZZ.

GYM

LOBBY

OFF.

FUTURE POOL

N

20

The concept of raised seating around an oval space for combat has changed since the time of the Roman Empire in all ways except the basic ones. Arenas continue to be places for a passive public's enjoyment of athletes in action, and the seating is still arranged around the center of interest. The ways in which arenas have changed are of utmost interest in the following pages. Modern developments include special arrangements to meet the special requirements of particular sports, sizes that meet the special needs of different promoters, and flexibility that allows different activities in the same space. The movement of large populations to the suburbs has resulted in better planning to handle traffic flow, and long span roofs to permit games during bad weather. The big question is the effect on future construction of a possible movement away from spectator sports.

The specialization of facilities for special sports is illustrated by every example on the following pages. The first project, Teletrack in New Haven, by Herbert S. Newman Associates, is not, strictly speaking, an arena at all. Rather it is a theater-in-the-round for watching horse races on closed-circuit television. While the ancient Romans would be surprised by such a facility for spectator sports, Teletrack illustrates one extreme of specialization that exists today through advances in technology.

The second project, the National Tennis Center by David Kenneth Spector is a more traditionally conceived arena for a sport that has not until recently been conducted in the presence of large numbers of intense spectators: tennis. Accordingly, this arena has the proper sightlines and orientation for this particular game, while representing another aspect of arena construction that may have implications for the future: an ingenious reuse of an existing stadium built for the 1964-1965 World's Fair. The third project, the new Olympic Center for Lake Placid by Hellmuth , Obata & Kassabaum meets the very special requirements of Olympic ice skating competition.

Another extreme of specialization is seen in the last project, the Milford Jai Alai, again by Herbert S. Newman Associates. Here, the center of attention, the court, is located to one side of the building to accommodate the special playing and safety requirements of the fast-moving, dangerous game. And there is a willful direction of spectators through the betting "lounges" to reach their seats.

While arenas may seem to be no exception to the trend towards larger and larger facilities of every kind, there is a maximum number of seats, about 20,000 for most athletic events, beyond which players will begin to appear as ants from the farthest seats. On these pages, only the National Tennis Center and the Special Events Center in Austin by Crain/Anderson approach this size.

Other factors beside sight distance tend to restrict the size of new facilities. These include the size of audiences that local promoters can expect to attract and the costs of building and maintaining really large facilities. Inevitably, the costs must be offset by the ability to use the large facilities for more than one purpose—as in Austin. Here, flexibility—the ability to use the same space for sports, theater and even banquets—is an important factor.

When the arenas are big, they produce a by-product, the need for large parking areas. Coupled with the pressures of rising land values in center city locations, the factors of circulation and parking almost dictate a movement to less congested locales.

Finally, there is the question of how many new arenas will be built. If current trends toward more participatory sports continue, there could be a dampening of enthusiasm for watching others in action—especially among younger generations. At least one thing is sure in the field of arenas, big may not always be better.

Chapter Seven

Arenas

TELETRACK
NEW HAVEN, CONNECTICUT
Herbert S. Newman Associates

"I am not such a guy as you will expect to find in New Haven at any time," declared one of Damon Runyon's Broadway horse players, a serious betting man who preferred to stay within easy reach of Aqueduct and Belmont Park. Times have changed, though, and New Haven is no longer terra incognita for followers of the sport of kings, thanks to 1976 legislation permitting pari-mutuel betting in Connecticut and the recent completion of Teletrack, "the world's first Theater of Racing."

Glimpsed from a car on the nearby Connecticut Turnpike, Teletrack's cylindrical amphitheater might briefly be mistaken for one of the oil storage tanks that dot the surrounding flatlands. But there's no chance of confusion as soon as one sights the flourish of neon graphics and festive signage that announce the building's horsy theme. Inside, a combination of closed-circuit television and computerized off-track betting enables 2,200 spectators to place wagers with Connecticut's OTB system while watching live thoroughbred racing—transmitted via microwave from five New York tracks and projected in full color on a 24-by 32-foot screen.

From the outset of the project, when his firm won a closed competition staged by the General Instrument Corporation (manufacturers of OTB and TV equipment), architect Herbert S. Newman conceived Teletrack as "a place where spectators can share their enjoyment of the event." The drama begins at the entrance canopy, where racing fans arrive in style under multicolored flags, and continues into a lobby whose sportive tone is set by neon horseshoes on the ceiling, photomurals of the track, and banners cut from jockeys' silks. Glassbrick "starting gates" house ticket booths and turnstiles.

Spectators are offered the choice of

Norman McGrath photos

160

At New Haven's $8-million Teletrack, video simulcasts of thoroughbred racing beamed in from New York State add a new dimension to offtrack betting. Supergraphics scaled for long-range visibility guide motorists to the porte-cochère (detail, upper left). Shallow ''rustication'' and a stepped grid of blind windows (photos left and right) articulate the geometric massing of betting lounges, restaurants, and circulation areas clustered around the drum-like amphitheater.

A 24- by 32-foot screen is the focus of the 1,800-seat grandstand, seen (above) from one of eight balconies in the second-tier Clubhouse. Plans of the three main levels show how the lobby, ramp, and stairway (photos right) wrap around the amphitheater to compose a dramatic entrance. Grandstand seating is aligned along an asymmetrical, fan-shaped layout that echoes the curve of the foyer—and points spectators in the direction of the betting lounge. A separate circulation system behind the auditorium ensures the security of money-handling operations and Teletrack offices (see ground-level plan).

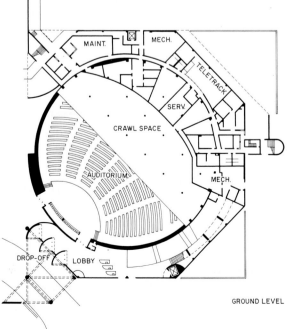

GROUND LEVEL

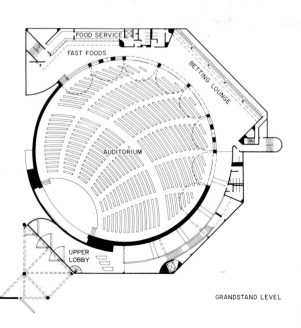

GRANDSTAND LEVEL

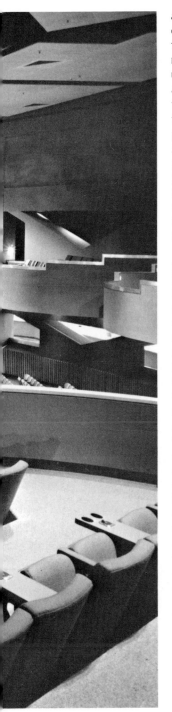

admission to an 1,800-seat grandstand, equipped with 29 betting windows and a fast-food counter, or the swankier—and more expensive—400-seat "Clubhouse" upstairs on the second tier. Clubhouse amenities include balconies overlooking the grandstand, the Winner's Circle restaurant, a separate betting lounge, and a panoramic view of New Haven harbor. Another story up, on the third tier, four private VIP Rooms flank the central projection booth. The electronic equipment that masterminds Teletrack's technical wizardry is tightly guarded in a ground-floor control area, with its own circulation system.

The ramp and stairway that lead the public along a ceremonial route from the lobby to the amphitheater make for a lively "post parade" before the main event. Like a pre-race warm-up, this carefully paced entry allows spectators' eyes to adjust gradually from daylight outside (most races are run in the afternoon or early evening) to the relative darkness required for film viewing—preventing a condition that project lighting consultant Sylvan R. Shemitz calls "Saturday matinée blindness." For maximum visibility within the theater, house lights are programmed to dim when a race is about to start, the screen is recessed to obviate glare, and an ingenious ventilating system keeps the projected image clear of smoke (used air is extracted under grandstand seats and recycled to HEPA filters and ceiling diffusers from a sub-floor plenum). The diehard traditionalist might insist on binoculars, but they are hardly necessary here: the circular plan brings most seats within comfortable viewing distance, and a clear span of steel beams (seven-foot-deep built-up plate girders) mounted on peripheral steel columns opens up a remarkable range of unobstructed sight-lines. Structural cross-bracing, which could have been a handicap to visibility, is put to

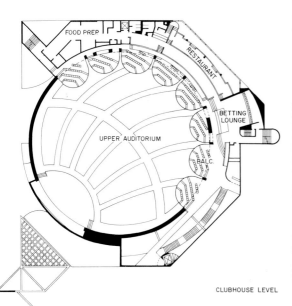

CLUBHOUSE LEVEL

good use as a frame for unexpected diagonal vistas from the VIP level and the fast-food bar. Acoustically efficient non-asbestos mineral fibers, sprayed onto the light steel-stud walls, help to temper the echoes of cheers—and groans—as the horses enter the homestretch.

Audience participation is the essence of pari-mutuel betting, and Herbert Newman believes that the bold geometry of Teletrack's central rotunda evokes "an archetypal sense of space that all sorts of people respond to with wonder and excitement." Between races, the warm russet of grandstand seating (repeated in the fabric covering of Clubhouse walls), the sweep of bow-front loges, and the jazzy zigzag-patterned ceiling create a vibrant background for trackside activity. The over-all effect is an amalgam of gaiety and monumentality, much as though a 1930s movie palace had been installed within a Roman arena. It's hardly a setting for the Ascot Gavotte, but judging by the enthusiastic crowds that keep Teletrack busy six days a week, this video hippodrome has captured the high spirits of the turf with a panache all its own.

TELETRACK, New Haven, Connecticut. Owner: *General Instrument Corporation.* Architects: *Herbert S. Newman Associates, AIA, PC—Herbert S. Newman, architect-in-charge; Don Cosham, associate, project manager; Bob Godshall, job captain; Hugh Sullivan, assistant.* Engineers: *Spiegel & Zamecnik, Inc.* (structure/foundations); *Helenski Associates, Inc.* (mechanical/electrical); *Bolt, Beranek, and Newman, Inc.* (acoustics); *Sylvan R. Shemitz & Associates, Inc.* (lighting); *James Skerritt/Lawrence Appleton* (landscaping); *C. E. Maguire, Inc.* (site engineers). Interior design: *Herbert S. Newman Associates—Herbert S. Newman, Glenn H. Gregg, Edna Newman.* Graphics: *Mary Ann Rumney.* General contractor: *E & F Construction Company.*

Architect Herbert Newman's design is calculated to appeal to a broad range of users, "so that racing fans on a tight budget won't be put off by too-rich surroundings, and the better-heeled won't feel they're slumming." From the colorful grandstand betting lounge (top left) to well-appointed VIP Rooms (above), Teletrack's amenities enhance the pleasure of anyone's day at the races. Diners in the Clubhouse restaurant can keep an eye on the horses—either on the big screen or on overhead monitors—without putting down their forks. The section (opposite) reveals the steel column-and-beam structure that encloses the arena's wide-open spaces (155 feet in diameter at the base of the grandstand).

164

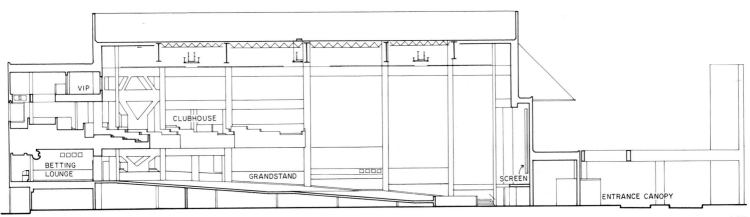

USTA NATIONAL TENNIS CENTER, FLUSHING MEADOW, NEW YORK
David Kenneth Specter

For the better part of this century, American tennis and Forest Hills seemed to be synonymous. The West Side Tennis Club—nestled amid the brick and Tudor houses of this tidy New York suburb—was the Mother Church of the sport (at least in America) and the scene each summer of a series of events that culminated in the staging of the U.S. National Championships. This was, of course, an event of considerable glamour and tradition, a tradition that was richly expressed in the West Side's handsome old half-timber clubhouse, its venerable stadium and its gracious expanse of beautifully manicured lawns. Even the surrounding community, built up around narrow, tree-lined streets with names like Dartmouth and Exeter, seemed to bestow an added measure of lordly dignity.

But even before 1968 when tennis began its great surge, Forest Hills had become a tight-fitting suit. After 1968, when the U.S. National Championship became the U.S. Open, American tennis needed a new home.

The new site, only a few miles from the old, was nevertheless very different in character. It centered on an all but derelict stadium left over from the 1964-65 World's Fair in Flushing Meadow. Originally called the Singer Bowl, later renamed after Louis Armstrong, the stadium was a shallow, rectangular tray ringed by a low grandstand of small capacity with most of its seating located too far from a potential center court—a court that would lie in the wrong axis for tennis anyway. But if the geometry was unpromising, the stadium was well

located with respect to transportation both public and private, and the surrounding space was more than ample.

These were among the considerations that USTA president Slew Hester and architect David Specter grappled with during feasibility studies. It was during one of these early meetings between Specter and structural engineer Ysrael Seinuk (principal in the Office of Irwin Cantor) that the idea of superimposing a new grandstand ring over a portion of the old stadium was first advanced. Obvious only in retrospect, it was an idea with powerful implications. It made it possible to bring large numbers of seats within comfortable viewing distance of a center court that could now be realigned north-south. And it left an existing area of seating to frame a smaller

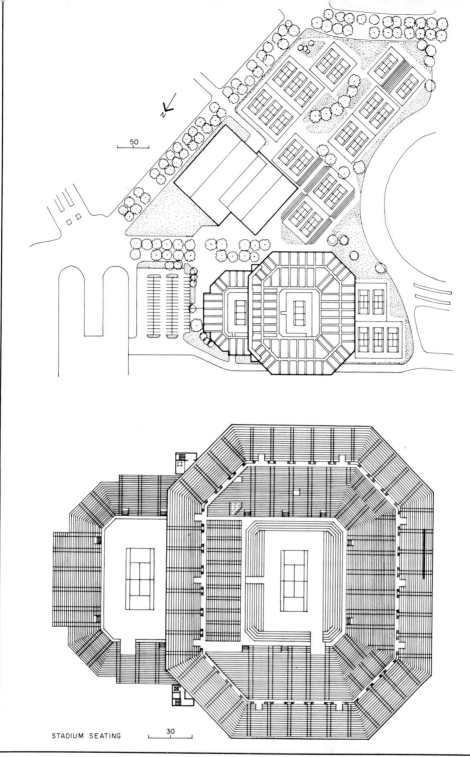

STADIUM SEATING $\vdash\quad 30\quad\dashv$

The extent of the new National Tennis Center is shown in the site plan and in the photo at upper left. The two structures of light industrial character to the left of the stadium house a total of nine air-conditioned, covered courts as well as locker rooms, lounges, restaurant, pro shop and administrative spaces. The Center also offers a total of 25 outdoor courts that during most of the year can be rented by the tennis-playing public.

secondary arena or "grandstand court." The decision was made to plunge ahead. Using fast-tracking techniques and a range of industrial materials and finishes, the project was brought to completion (or at least to a satisfactory level of completion) in the remarkably brief period of 10 months, a tribute not only to the architect but to USTA officials, responsible city agencies, and construction crews alike.

As built, the new stadium addition is structurally independent of the existing grandstand. Together they provide seating for just under 20,000 spectators in the main stadium with an additional 6,000 in the grandstand arena. (At the West Side Tennis Club, the seating capacity was between 14,000 and 15,000). Access to the new facility is easy and

167

on-site circulation routes are clearly developed.

Many of the problems that inevitably arise in a large new facility of this kind were solved in the first two years of shakedown. Of those that remained, the most vexing resulted from the Center's location under a major air-traffic approach to nearby La Guardia Airport. The loud drone of low flying aircraft overhead is a continuing annoyance to players, spectators and broadcasters. A minor but continuing controversy also centers on the character of the playing surfaces. The courts are finished in *Deco Turf II,* a rubber-fortified, elastormeric coating over an asphalt base. Some prominent players argue that the surface is ''too fast'' and penalizes those players who learned the game on the

168

slower clay surfaces of Europe. It should be noted, however, that no court surface yet developed suits everybody, and that this surface was selected only after a thorough poll of player preferences. Apart from the question of surface, tournament players give the new facility high marks. They enjoy a privacy here that they never had at Forest Hills and the number of practice courts available for their use is generous.

One of the most important features of the new Center—and one that distinguishes it sharply from the West Side Tennis Club—is that for 10 months of the year, the Center is a public facility and adds importantly to the slender inventory of local, rentable courts. Under terms of an agreement worked out between the USTA and the City, the USTA

has exclusive use of the Center for 60 days each year and control during this period of all incoming revenues. For this, it maintains the facility year-round and pays the City a guaranteed annual minimum of $125,000. It is a happy arrangement for both parties and one that could and might serve well as a model for cooperation between the public and private sectors everywhere.

NATIONAL TENNIS CENTER, Flushing Meadow, New York: Architect and graphic designer: *David Kenneth Specter*—(*Rodger Braley, John Van Fossen: project team*. Engineers: *Office of Irwin Cantor* (structural); *Flack & Kurtz* (consulting). Landscape architects: *The Schnadelbach-Braun Partnership*. Directory: *Wade Zimmerman*. Construction manager: *Leonard Borgida, HRH Construction Co.*

Norman McGrath

Wolfgang Hoyt

Dramatic in its massing and forthright in its execution and finishes, the new Center has become for some traditionalists a symbol for the changes that have come to tennis during the past decade. For these critics, the casting off of the game's elitist image (as symbolized by the move from Forest Hills) was a fall from grace itself. For others, however, the Center is a fitting expression of the sport's new strength and popular support.

Wolfgang Hoyt

Austin American-Statesman/Lou Cooper

SPECIAL EVENTS CENTER, UNIVERSITY OF TEXAS, AUSTIN, TEXAS
Crain/Anderson

The Superdrum, as the Special Events Center is affectionately called by those who use it, is a remarkably flexible entertainment space. During one seven-day period in early 1979, for example, this facility was host to six large-scale events. The sequence began with a 2,000-guest banquet and dance. The next day crowds were treated to a show by the Royal Lippizan Stallions. Two days later, the University of Texas basketball team beat Rice. Right after the game, the floor was picked up and the proscenium erected to accommodate a performance of *The Wiz*. The following day, the floor went back down for the Harlem Globetrotters who were followed in turn an evening later by Boston, the popular rock group. In the two years since it opened, in fact, the Special Events Center has hosted ice

shows, circuses, symphonic and operatic performances, university convocations, commencement exercises, major political addresses—just about every sort of large-scale event to which the greater Austin community could be attracted. This community includes approximately 300,000 people.

The basic enclosure is a drum with a base diameter of 402 feet and a height of 97 feet. The steel structure is clad in buff-colored precast panels and it rests on a large podium or terrace that serves as the main access to the building. Twenty-eight feet below terrace level is the 24,000-square-foot arena floor. This floor is surrounded by two tiers of seats with a combined capacity of 16,200. For theatrical events, the space can be arranged for theater-in-the-round or for conventional

stage by erecting a proscenium arch as shown in the photo next page. This configuration produces a stage that is 96 by 60 feet and enclosed by a system of tall drapes that can be stored when not in use. Lights and scenery can be flown in from a 32-lineset grid system overhead.

The seating plan is essentially a series of concentric ovals inscribed within the circular plan of the drum. This arrangement provides more seating along the long sides of the playing area and therefore better viewing angles for more of the seats. By masking certain sections of the seating and retracting others, a wide variety of arrangements can be achieved.

In a structure with such a high level of convertibility, the acoustical system had to be

170

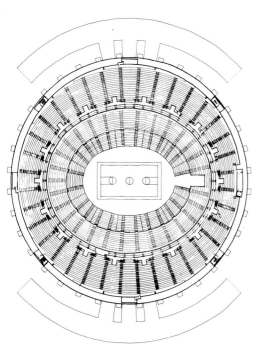

Richard Payne photos except as noted

carefully engineered. It consists of two banks of speaker clusters that provide uniform sound coverage to the arena floor and the lower tiers of seats. The upper-level seating rings are equipped with digital delay devices on a separate speaker system, a condition that minimizes reverberation and echo. To complement the sound reinforcement system, the architects have installed perforated metal walls with fiberglass backing behind the upper tier, a suspended acoustical ceiling (also over the upper tier), carpeted walls and fully upholstered seats.

The Special Events Center has two distinct lighting systems. The first, for sports events, is itself highly flexible. It consists of 288 1000-Watt halogen lamps mounted on a high catwalk overhead and angled so that there is no spill or glare to spectators. These units can be modulated according to the requirements of the events from boxing, which is tightly focused on a small area, to rodeo which extends to the full perimeter of the arena.

The theater lighting, designed by Abe Feder to accommodate either proscenium or arena stage, includes 96 ellipsoidal spotlights, border lighting and eight cradles of quartz lamps used as side lighting. Provision is also made for a range of portable units to be used when any of a variety of special effects is desired.

The very variety of events, their size and level of activity, required the deployment of a sophisticated and carefully zoned air distribution system that automatically maintains a 72 degree temperature at 55 per cent relative humidity.

In the first two years of its operation, this extraordinary facility has been highly successful. Unlike some other multi-purpose arenas—where only a fraction of their designed versatility is ever utilized—the flexibility of the Special Events Center has been continuously challenged and the challenge has been met again and again.

SPECIAL EVENTS CENTER, Austin, Texas. Architects: *Crain/Anderson, Inc.—project team: John K. Anderson, Robert J. Minchew* Engineers: *Walter P. Moore & Associates* (structural); *Cook & Holle* (mechanical). Consultants: *Lighting by Feder* (lighting); *Bouer & Associates* (acoustical). Contractor: *H.A. Lott.*

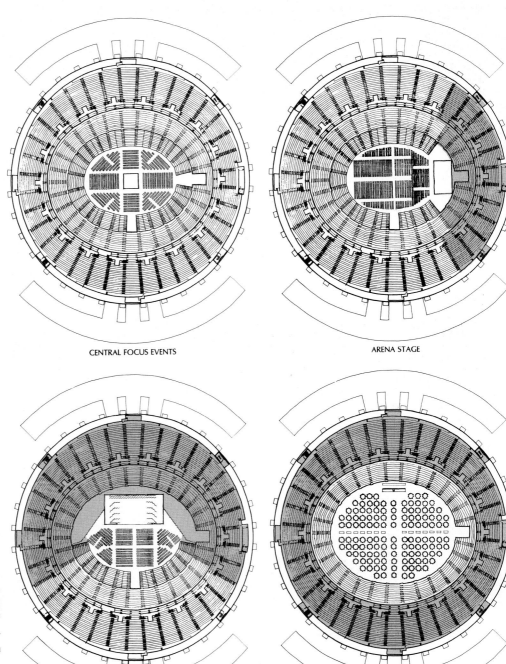

CENTRAL FOCUS EVENTS

ARENA STAGE

PROSCENIUM STAGE

BANQUETS

Four basic seating arrangements—each tailored to a particular kind of event—are shown in diagrammatic form above. In the section below and in the photo at left, the arena is set for theater. The focus is a 40- by 60-foot proscenium opening. Most conversions of the facility can be accomplished in a day.

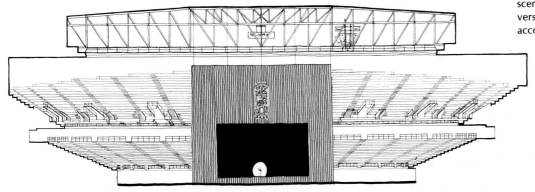

The roof of the arena is framed in a two-way steel truss system of sufficient depth to create a mechanical attic 28 feet high at its midpoint. These trusses span

386 feet and house a system of catwalks that provide access to the lighting and to the theatrical rigging and hoists shown in the several photos above and at right. The rigging process is facilitated by the design of a 30-foot-wide ramp at the buildings south end, a ramp on which trucks can drive right on to the arena floor to load and unload.

OLYMPIC CENTER, LAKE PLACID, NEW YORK
Helmuth, Obata & Kassabaum

Years of planning and building were crowned when 1400 athletes and an estimated 45,000 spectators descended on this picturesque Adirondack town and joined in celebrating the XIII Winter Olympic Games. It was not the first time Lake Placid has hosted the Games. In 1932, at the lowpoint of the Depression, this upstate community staged the III Olympic Winter Games in what was, for then, sumptuous style. But in the years since, the Winter Games have grown and prospered to the point that the 1932 ice arena—the arena in which 19-year-old Sonja Henie won a gold medal—was far from adequate and organizers of the 1980 Games commissioned Helmuth, Obata & Kassabaum to design a new arena.

The new building stands just to the

southwest of the old and is joined to it by a shared entry. Together they comprise the largest and best equipped indoor skating facility anywhere. The new program requirements included a 30-meter by 60-meter Olympic-sized ice sheet as well as a second sheet dimensioned to somewhat smaller United States standards which, during the Games, saw service as a practice arena and as a competition surface for skater's school figures. Both arenas are served by an extensive complex of dressing rooms, cafeteria, and related support and administrative spaces.

The building's most striking visual feature —and this is the image that Olympic televiewers were most likely to absorb and retain—is the series of eleven trusses that run

vertically down the south face of the building, giving this elevation a very lively geometry both in form and shadow pattern. On the exterior, the trusses, made up of WF sections, are tied together to provide a lateral stiffness. Inside, the trusses span the main arena, a span of 240 feet, and their depth is sufficient to accommodate mechanical services and suspended walkways that give access to the lighting. Inside is a grandstand structure that is entirely independent of the exterior system of trusses and insulated metal panels. The two systems, though they remain structurally separate, interlock visually in the glass-enclosed stairways on the building's exterior. From these stairways, views of the adjacent speed-skating oval and the surrounding region are quite spectacular.

Bill Remington

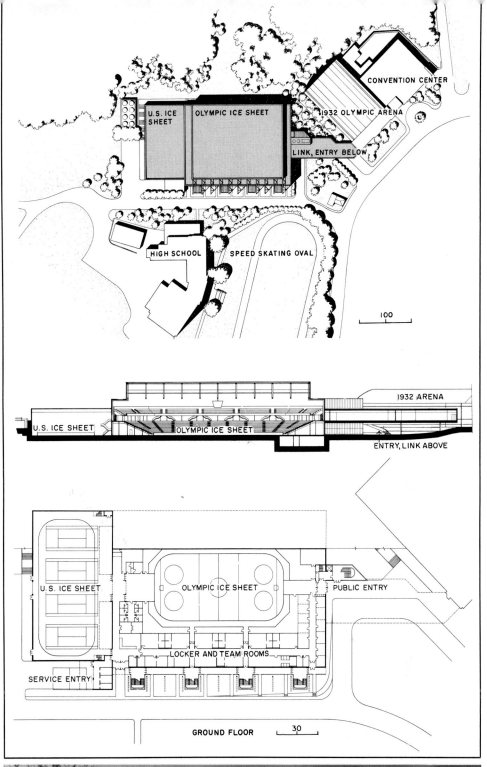

CONVENTION CENTER

U.S. ICE SHEET   OLYMPIC ICE SHEET   1932 OLYMPIC ARENA

LINK, ENTRY BELOW

HIGH SCHOOL   SPEED SKATING OVAL

100

1932 ARENA

U.S. ICE SHEET   OLYMPIC ICE SHEET

ENTRY, LINK ABOVE

U.S. ICE SHEET   OLYMPIC ICE SHEET   PUBLIC ENTRY

LOCKER AND TEAM ROOMS

SERVICE ENTRY

GROUND FLOOR   30

Fitted with care into a tight site, the new Olympic Center is seen above as a backdrop to the new refrigerated speed skating oval. The Center occupies a hillside site between the 1932 arena and the Lake Placid High School.

George Cserna

177

George Silk photos except as noted

The main public access and circulation for the Olympic arena is at the concourse level. From this level, spectators descend into one or another of the 5000 permanent seats that surround the ice sheet. Bleachers placed above the concourse level added 3000 "temporary" seats for the Games. Athletes have separate circulation routes at ice level. During the Olympic events, response from both participants and spectators was approving. The sight lines are excellent and skaters appreciate the generous dimensions of the rink as well as the general ambience of color and light. It was the task of Jules Fisher & Paul Marantz to design lighting that would serve the facility effectively for the variety of smaller scale events that followed the Olympics. This they accomplished using a range of high-intensity, metal halide installations over the competition areas and fluorescent fixtures elsewhere. Some special lighting in the form of colored ice washers and spots is also included, but a good deal of the special lighting required for color television transmission was brought in for the Games by broadcasters. It is hoped by all those concerned that, after the Games, Lake Placid will be not only an Olympic training center—where a new generation of skaters and skiers can be coached to international standards—but also a mecca for winter vacationers and sportsmen of every caliber. If that happens, it will boost the region's chronically weak economy. At the same time, it will test the flexibility of this fine new arena by providing it with a variety of events from trade shows to cultural programs of many kinds. The budget for the Olympic Center was $11,500,000 plus 10 per cent for contingencies. Hellmuth, Obata & Kassabaum brought the building in on budget in spite of the fact that certain redesign was required when the original steel contractor went bankrupt and had to be replaced.

OLYMPIC CENTER, Lake Placid, New York. Architects: *Hellmuth, Obata & Kassabaum*—project team: *Gyo Obata, Gerard Gilmore, Harry Culpen, John Way, Terry Harkness, Charles Reay.* Engineers: *Jack D. Gillum & Associates* (structural); *Cosentini Associates* (mechanical/electrical); *Ahrendt Engineering* (refrigeration). Acoustical consultant: *Robert A. Hansen Associates;* lighting design: *Jules Fisher & Paul Marantz, Inc.* Construction manager: *Gilbane Building Company.*

178

Much controversy centered on the structural design—specifically the design of the roof trusses. The failures of several roof systems that were faintly similar led to allegations of structural inadequacy first voiced by a member of the Lake Placid Economic Development Administration. Two investigations by independent engineering offices led to minor changes that could easily be accommodated within the system. With their completion, the controversy subsided.

MILFORD JAI ALAI MILFORD, CONNECTICUT
Herbert S. Newman Associates

Norman McGrath photos

The main entrance to the Milford fronton is under a bright yellow translucent canopy supported on a wood truss system. Its open glass wall offers approaching visitors a sense of the brightness and color inside. The photo below shows the elevation at the rear of the grandstand, with its secondary entrance from the self-parking area. This view expresses the huge trusses which span 180 feet across the grandstand-playing court area (from right in photo) and then cantilever another 60 feet beyond the column line to roof the galleria and restaurant areas. At the far left in the photo is the International Room (see plan). The plan is described in detail in the text opposite. The 150,000-square-foot building is on a 21-acre site with parking for 2000 cars set on terraces of the hillside. Building cost: $9.2 million.

At Milford Jai Alai there are two main entrances—the valet parking entrance shown in the photo right, and a secondary entrance for those who park their own cars (below). Connecting these two entrances is the "galleria"—best seen on the level 1 plan. This grand space is the key both to the functioning of and circulation within the whole facility—and to the sense of festivity which this building so strongly projects.

From the main entrance level, the gallery steps up two levels corresponding to the slope of the site and the spectator grandstand. This space can be seen in the vertical photo on the next spread, and several other pictures suggest its importance to the plan. Moving through the space under colorful banners, visitors can (see plans) move into a 250-seat restaurant and bar to their right, or into betting lounge number 1 to the left. Beyond that, the first step of an escalator leads up to an intermediate level, with a small bar to the right and betting lounge number 2. The second flight of escalators leads to level 3. Off its lobby there is the secondary (self-park) entrance; to the right a 10,000-square-foot International Room which offers refreshments and closed-circuit television displaying the games via a 12- by 15-foot rear projection screen; and to the left, betting lounge number 3.

The grandstand (unless you really take a long way around) can only be entered via one of the betting lounges (clever, what?) tucked under grandstand seating above. From these broad spaces—with betting windows on one side, concession stands on the other—the seats of that level are reached by vomitoria. Conversely, from any seat in the grandstand, it is a very short walk to the pari-mutuel window of your choice. (The typical "game" in jai alai takes 12 minutes, and the 12 games played each night are separated by 15 minute intervals—long enough to place your next bet.)

The grandstand (top photo, next page) seats 4800 in an unobstructed space 180 feet wide. This space is spanned by exposed steel trusses 30 feet on center which cantilever 60 feet beyond the grandstand space to form the roof of the galleria and restaurant spaces and extend beyond as a sunshade. The seats slope up following the contours of the hillside site. The focus of everything, of course, is the playing court—180 feet long, 50 feet wide, 48

feet high, bright green, and lighted to a level of 176 footcandles at the center of the court. The unique and ingenious lighting— conceived by consultant Sylvan Shemitz—is totally indirect, avoiding any glare in the eyes of the players when they look up. It utilizes 60 luminaires, 30 on each side of the court at six-foot intervals, which create an asymmetric distribution of light washing the ceiling plane uniformly. There are three other engineering/construction features that contribute greatly to the design success of the building: 1) the beautifully integrated structural system by engineer (and former Yale dean of architecture) Herman Spiegel, 2) the extraordinary accomplishment of the general contractor in pouring the court surfaces plumb and smooth in one pass, and 3) the innovative use of "Dryvit"—an insulating exterior finishing system with integral signing and supergraphics.

There are of course special and specialized areas which the architect had to work into the complex: the offices, players' rooms, and the pari-mutuel department. Given the large amounts of money handled each night, this area is of course highly secure, and its circulation is entirely separate from the public. But in the public spaces, the mood created by architect Newman's planning and design is "the festival": the noise and excitement of the fans in the grandstand pours into the great galleria and even into the bars and restaurants beyond. So everywhere in the building the excitement and color of the game is heightened by the excitement and color generated by the design.

MILFORD JAI ALAI, Milford, Connecticut. Owner: *Saturday Corporation*. Architects: *Herbert S. Newman Associates, AIA, PC—Herbert S. Newman, partner-in-charge; project architects: Glen H. Gregg, partner and William P. Newhall, associate; Don Cosham and Joseph Schiffer, associates; Robert Godshall and Jan Van Loan, assistants.* Engineers: *Spiegel & Zamecnik, Inc. (structure and foundations); Helenski Associates, Inc. (mechanical and electrical); Bolt, Beranek and Newman, Inc. (acoustics); Sylvan R. Shemitz & Associates, Inc. (lighting); CMA Partnership (landscaping); Mary Ann Rumney, Graphic Design (graphics).* General contractor: *George B. M. Macomber Company*.

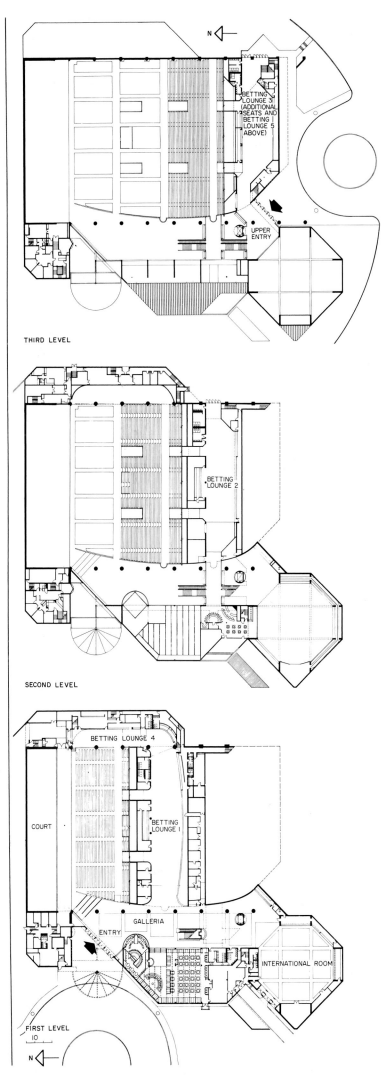

THIRD LEVEL

SECOND LEVEL

FIRST LEVEL

Inside, all is color and brightness and festivity. At far left, the great galleria, as seen from the main entrance, with the escalators to the upper levels at the rear. The yellow cylinder offers alternate elevator travel. Neon is used not just for signing (as at the entrance to the bar and restaurant at the right) but in stylish supergraphics throughout the space. A section of the bar, sheltered from but still open to the crowds and color and noise outside, is shown near left. Above, is the 4800-seat grandstand, which is as wide as the 180-foot playing surface. Below, photos show how the grandstand space opens to the galleria, so those moving around "feel as if they are standing in a street next to an open stadium of cheering fans." Below right: A view from an upper level of the restaurant.

Index